MINI CASES IN MARKETING

The Marketing Series is one of the most comprehensive collections of textbooks in marketing and sales available from the UK today.

Published by Heinemann Professional Publishing on behalf of the Chartered Institute of Marketing, the series has been specifically designed, developed and progressively updated over a number of years to support students studying for the Institutes certificate and diploma qualifications. The scope of the subjects covered by the series, however, means that it is of equal value to anyone studying other further or higher business and/or marketing related qualifications.

Formed in 1911, the Chartered Institute of Marketing is now the largest professional marketing managment body in Europe with over 22,000 members and 25,000 students located worldwide. Its primary objectives are focused on the development of awareness and understanding of marketing throughout UK industry and commerce and in the raising of standards of professionalism in the education, training and practice of this key business discipline.

Other titles in the series

Mini Cases
in
Marketing

Lester Massingham

Principal, MTMS Limited and Senior Examiner
to the Institute of Marketing

and

Geoff Lancaster

University of Newcastle-upon-Tyne
and Senior Examiner to the Institute of
Marketing and Chief Examiner to the London
Chamber of Commerce and Industry

Published on behalf of the
Chartered Institute of Marketing

 PART OF REED INTERNATIONAL BOOKS
OXFORD   LONDON   GUILDFORD   BOSTON
MUNICH   NEW DELHI   SINGAPORE   SYDNEY
TOKYO   TORONTO   WELLINGTON

Butterworth-Heinemann Ltd
Halley Court, Jordan Hill, Oxford OX2 8EJ

First published 1990
Reprinted 1991

British Library Cataloguing in Publication Data
Massingham, Lester
  Mini cases in marketing.
  1. Marketing
  I. Title   II. Lancaster, Geoffrey A.   III. Chartered Institute of
    Marketing
  658.8

ISBN 0 7506 0171 X
Printed in Great Britain by Billing & Sons Ltd, Worcester

CONTENTS

ACKNOWLEDGEMENTS

Our thanks must go to staff from the Chartered Institute of Marketing and to Norman Waite in particular, without whose cooperation and help this text would not have been possible.

More specifically, our thanks must also go to senior examiners of the Chartered Institute of Marketing for allowing us to use their case studies as practical exercises which has added realism to this text, because such case studies have been tried out in practice in real examination situations.

Senior examiners whom we would like to specifically thank are David Pearson, Keith Crosier and Frank Harthill.

1

INTRODUCTION

1.1 The need for this text

The text has been designed and written specifically to help students of marketing tackle 'mini-case studies'. This form of examining is becoming increasingly popular for examining marketing in first degree and diploma courses and many higher degree courses.

Such examining was pioneered by the Chartered Institute of Marketing when it introduced the mini-case concept into its final diploma subjects:

- International aspects of marketing;
- Marketing communications;
- Marketing management – planning and control.

More recently, it has introduced the mini-case approach to certificate subjects:

- Practice of sales management;
- Practice of marketing.

This book is therefore invaluable to Chartered Institute of Marketing students who are preparing for their certificate and diploma examinations, and it is from previous Chartered Institute of Marketing papers that the majority of examples used throughout this book have been taken. A step-by-step guide is provided to take students through the nature of mini cases and help them prepare and present answers to problems set by examiners.

The text is also invaluable to any students of marketing where the mini-case format is used for examining purposes. Much reliance has been placed upon Chartered Institute of Marketing material because its past papers have produced a large database that is divided into a number of specialist marketing subdivisions. The reality, therefore, is that after having worked through this book, any student of marketing should be able to confidently tackle an examination that uses a mini-case format.

1.2   The structure of the text

We start with a brief examination of the background to the reasons for the introduction of mini cases to the Chartered Institute of Marketing diploma examinations. By analysing these reasons, it is possible to provide a number of clues as to what examiners are looking for from mini-case examination candidates.

In the next part of the text you are introduced to the format and structure of those diploma examinations which contain a mini case, noting the important points about the format of these cases. This process is continued by comparing and contrasting the mini-case papers with the maxi-case paper of the Chartered Institute of Marketing – the three hour 'open-book' examination called marketing management (analysis and decision). This is very important and useful, because all too often candidates fail to appreciate that the mini-case approach is *different* to that required for the analysis and decision case.

By this point in the text, you will then be in a position to summarize some of the first learning points about tackling mini-case studies.

The text goes on to develop a framework for tackling mini cases, summarizing some of the key points to remember when preparing answers. In order to underline the importance of these key points, we have included an analysis of examiners' comments on recent mini cases in order to illustrate some of the more common criticisms of mini-case candidates.

The next section of the text takes you through detailed worked examples of how to tackle a mini case: one for each of the diploma subjects in which the mini-case format is used. These worked examples are designed to illustrate how the previous learning points work when practising working through a mini case.

By this time you are ready to tackle mini cases in a mock examination situation. Diploma mini cases are included, covering each of the diploma areas. These are followed by 'specimen' answers in order that you can evaluate how your answer compares with an 'expert' answer. In order to obtain the maximum value from these examples, you are advised to work through the cases on your own, preferably under self imposed examination conditions before reading the specimen answer.

Finally, certificate mini cases are examined and analysed in a similar way, but the emphasis here is more upon tactics than strategy.

Throughout the text examples are provided without specimen answers to enable you to practise 'typical' mini-case problems without the security (and feeling of complacency) that might arise when a model answer is available.

2

BACKGROUND TO THE MINI-CASE FORMAT

2.1 Development

It is some years since the Chartered Institute of Marketing first introduced the short- or mini-case method of examining to the diploma examinations. In preparing yourself for this type of examination it is essential to understand the reasons for their introduction.

The diploma examinations constitute the final stage in becoming formally qualified as a marketing professional. Anyone who holds the diploma qualification must, therefore, possess the necessary skills and knowledge to act in a professional marketing capacity. This fact is now 'officially' recognized, because in 1988 the then Institute of Marketing received its Royal Charter and became the Chartered Institute of Marketing.

More than ever, today's professional marketer needs to be equipped with an in-depth knowledge of concepts and techniques needed to practise his or her profession. This should include an up-to-date knowledge of research and academic progress in the subject.

However, marketing is not just an academic discipline: it is a management function. As such, anyone claiming to be a skilled marketing professional must be able to demonstrate that they can apply their skills and knowledge to 'real life' marketing problems. Moreover, and again as in real life, the marketing professional must often demonstrate these application skills in the context of imperfect or at least incomplete information and within strict and often tight time schedules.

Before the introduction of the mini-case format, diploma examinations used the standard academic essay-type questions where candidates were required to demonstrate their knowledge and understanding of concepts and techniques, rather than an ability to apply such knowledge in a practical context. Quite rightly, the Institute recognized that their qualification is, in a sense a licence to practise, and then chose the mini-case format through which to test this.

That is the background to why the mini-case format was introduced and it begins to point to what this text covers; explaining the skills and fostering the approach required by candidates to tackle the mini-case parts of the examinations.

2.2 Application

Before we begin to specify precisely what these skills are, and particularly in order to clarify the necessary approach to the mini cases, we first need to examine the 'typical' structure and format of the mini case.

To do this, we have reproduced in full the international aspects of marketing paper from the June 1987 diploma examinations. You should read through this paper at least twice, noting the instructions to candidates and the time allocations for section of the paper and indeed, times that you will then be able to allocate to individual questions. You should also note the type of questions asked on the mini-case part of the paper.

Do not attempt, at this stage, to analyse the mini case or put forward your solutions, because the text goes on to analyse the format of this 'typical' question paper in some detail later, and notes all the important points to which you will need to pay attention when dealing with the mini-case format.

Diploma in Marketing

INTERNATIONAL ASPECTS OF MARKETING

Time: 09.30–12.30   Monday, 15 June, 1987
3 hours duration

This examination is divided into two distinct parts:
SECTION I *IS COMPULSORY CARRYING 50% OF THE MARKS FOR THE WHOLE PAPER. Candidates are advised, therefore, to budget their time accordingly allocating about 1½ hours to this part.*

SECTION II *requires you to answer THREE questions ONLY. You should read ALL the questions carefully before making your choice. All questions IN THIS SECTION carry equal marks.*

In both sections you should define your terms and give factual reasons to support your arguments. DO NOT repeat the questions in your answers but show clearly the section AND numbers of questions answered on appropriate pages of the answer book. Rough workings should be included in the answer book and neatly deleted after use.

INTERNATIONAL ASPECTS

Approximate time: 1½ hours   June 1987

Trade Gifts Ltd

Section I

Trade Gifts Ltd were wholesale suppliers of a wide range of presents and novelties which were bought by firms and organizations to give to suitable clients as gifts. Inscribed with the donor firm's name or logo as required, they could range from inexpensive pens, pencils, notepads, diaries or other desk top novelties, which could thereby be expected to keep the giver's name in front of the client as a reminder; up to more expensive items such as wallets, briefcases and calculators of various sorts, which could also be personalized with the recipient's initials or other insignia. Similarly, for use as free handouts at exhibitions or trade fairs, a variety of key rings, paper caps or simple toys could be provided for a client as a form of promotion.

The peak time of the year for the giving of these presents in the UK was at Christmas, but naturally the requirement for individual firms' promotions or trade fair attendance could occur at any time of the year. Although there were several organizations in the UK providing a similar range of supplies, Trade Gifts Ltd had recognized the potential of this market some 15 years ago, and had expanded their original business of office stationery suppliers to the gift business to the extent of having some 20% of the UK market for such items, and a turnover of some £5m in 1986. All the items featured in their catalogue were bought in from individual manufacturers, who also actually inscribed them; if not, Trade Gifts could subcontract this stage of the process, and these were then sold in bulk to the client for his distribution. Depending on the quantities ordered of each particular item, discounts were given according to order size.

Timing was, of course, critical. Whilst relatively small stocks of the more popular basic lines were kept for small, or rush, orders, even then there was still a time factor for them to be inscribed and delivered. There was also the problem of the ability of the manufacturer to supply larger quantities. If a deadline was missed, a dissatisfied client could quite possibly sue Trade Gifts for non-compliance with agreed conditions and consequential losses and Trade Gifts could be left with a quantity of unsellable merchandise.

When the board of Trade Gifts Ltd reviewed the 1986 results, they noted that while their market share had remained virtually constant, their profits had declined. Not only had competition become more fierce than previously, so that they had to reduce their margins, but also client firms were tending to cut back on the amount of money to be spent on such gifts, especially as the most expensive ones could possibly be seen as a form of bribe. Although Trade Gifts would not be legally involved in any such proceedings, the possibility could affect the range of products which they had available in this area, and which gave them their bigger margins.

Faced with this situation, one of the board members suggested the possibility of considering the provision of their service abroad, and it was agreed to investigate this approach further, as a matter of some urgency.

Questions

Advise Trade Gifts Ltd on the following three areas. Credit will be given for relevant additional observations and proposals.

(a) An outline research procedure to find suitable overseas market(s).
(b) Your recommendations for their most appropriate methods of entry to a selected market.
(c) Your proposals for publicity and promotion to support the entry.

All questions carry equal marks.

Section II   Approximate time: 1½ hours

Answer **three** *questions only*

1 (Global aspects)
The international marketer acts as an agent of cultural change, sometimes for the better, sometimes for the worse. Discuss.
2 (Organization)
How may the international marketing task of the exporter differ from that of an organization with wholly owned foreign production facilities?
3 (Logistics)
Discuss how different modes of transport may affect the packing and packaging of a particular export item.

4 (Product line policy)
Why is a firm's international product line unlikely to be identical to the domestic line? What could be the determinants of a firm's product line in a given foreign market?

5 (Product strategy – multinationals)
The multinational firm may have an advantage over the domestic firm in the generation of new product lines. Discuss how this may arise, and how the multinational may take advantage of such a situation.

6 (Representation)
Why is great care necessary in choosing a firm's representatives in a foreign market? What procedure might be followed in selecting foreign distributors?

7 (Exporting and barriers)
Outline the benefits possible for an international marketer to obtain by operating through a free trade zone.

8 (Pricing)
When setting a price for an export order to a customer in a foreign country, how could a supplier deal with (*1*) inflation and (*2*) significant currency fluctuations in that country?

2.3 Notes on format and structure

This paper on the international aspects of marketing syllabus is typical of the structure and format with which you can expect to be confronted in each of the three papers where a mini-case section is included. There are a number of points which you should note from our example.

2.3.1 *Sectionalization of paper/instructions to candidates*

You will note that the examination paper is divided into two distinct sections, with Section I being the mini case and Section II the more traditional essay type/discussion questions. You will also note that in Section I, the mini case *normally constitutes 50 per cent of the marks* for the paper and the *questions are compulsory*.

It is vital therefore that you follow the instructions carefully, *particularly with respect to suggested time allocation* for each section. Clearly, with 50 per cent of the marks being allocated for each section you need to divide your time approximately equally between the sections, i.e., 1½ hours each.

2.3.2 *Content of the mini cases*

Obviously the content of the mini cases is different for each subject and for each examination. What you should note, however, is that the mini case is not really a case at all; it is more an outline of a given business situation or a scenario. Hence, the information contained in mini cases tends to be much more focused according to the particular subject of each examination, than that found in, say, the open-book maxi-case study for analysis and decision. This and other differences between the mini- and maxi-case studies are important and are, therefore, explored in more depth later in this chapter.

2.3.3 *Number of questions and mark allocation*

In the example shown from the June 1987 paper, candidates were asked to answer three questions: (*a*), (*b*) and (*c*) on the mini case. The paper also specified that all questions in Section II carried equal marks. As with the sectionalization of the paper overall, you should be careful to follow these instructions carefully and allocate your time accordingly to each of the questions on the mini case. Normally, the mark allocation is a sound guide to the time allocation, but this is not always the case. Indeed, this particular paper only indicates that 50 per cent of the total marks for the paper are allocated to the mini case. Each question should, therefore, be treated on its own merits, but since different marks are not given it is reasonably safe to assume that each question will be scored equally.

You should note that the precise question format for the mini cases and, indeed, the number of questions you may be asked has, in the past, varied between subjects and from year to year. However, it is now normal for the mini-case section to have *three* questions with *equal* marks for each question. Where no indication of the mark allocation between questions is given, you should assume an equal mark allocation and state this assumption on your examination paper.

You should also note that in the particular example shown, candidates were informed that any *relevant* additional observations and proposals would be credited. This is quite normal procedure in mini cases, and you should not hesitate to add such material. The key word is *relevant*, and you should not see this as an opportunity to go off at a tangent, or digress into an inappropriate area of discussion. First, make sure that you have covered the questions set. Only then are you in a position to earn bonus marks through additional insights.

2.3.4 *Answer format for mini cases*

An essay type format is usually inappropriate for answering mini-case questions. Very often the precise format required in an answer will be specified in the questions themselves, with report and/or memorandum type formats being particularly favoured. Clearly, you should again follow the instructions closely as to the required format for the answer. Owing to the prevalence of report/memo type formats in the mini-case questions, these are explained in greater detail later in the text.

Now we need to explore further the crucial differences between the mini case and the maxi extended analysis and decision case.

3

DIFFERENCES BETWEEN MINI CASES AND THE MAXI CASE (ANALYSIS AND DECISION)

If mini cases were exactly the same as the extended maxi-case study, there would really be no point in having them. The most obvious difference is in terms of *length* of mini cases compared with the analysis and decision case, together with the amount of information you have to work upon. In addition, there are a number of other important distinctions between these short cases and the maxi case.

1   The mini-case examination is unseen. Unlike the analysis and decision case, you will only be presented with the actual mini case in the examination itself. This, of course, means that you have very little time in which to ascertain the most relevant details. In reality, the issues tend to be far less complex, and it must be remembered that all candidates are similarly disadvantaged.

2   Because these cases are so much shorter than the analysis and decision cases you will not be expected, nor indeed will it be possible, to prepare sophisticated and extended financial and statistical analyses and related techniques for these mini cases. This is not to say that you should ignore any financial or statistical information provided in the case: if it is there, it is probably there for a reason. The maxi case, on the other hand, often contains data which is not strictly relevant to the problems set because this type of case is usually based upon a factual situation –

some of which is relevant and some of which is irrelevant. It is normally the situation when preparing a mini case that the questions are set at the same time that the case material is prepared, so it is more likely that these questions relate directly to the case. On the other hand, maxi cases are written and the questions are set afterwards. In some situations it is not uncommon to have a 'standard' maxi case and for a number of questions to be generated from this case to be set at different examination sittings. In other words, the prose remains the same, but the questions are different. It must, however, be pointed out that the Chartered Institute of Marketing has not yet done this with its analysis and decision case, but other organizations have done it in their case study examinations and, indeed, we can see no harm in doing this.

3   The principal difference in analysis is that mini cases are concerned with proposing action plans for marketing and are not about the provision of extended analyses.

4   A final point is not so much an absolute difference between mini cases and the analysis and decision case, but is more one of emphasis. A feature of past Chartered Institute of Marketing mini cases is that a significant proportion feature small and sometimes relatively in-experienced companies, inexperienced would-be exporters, small businesses with a sole principal and so on. This is not to say that this will always be the situation.

As marketing applications develop and expand, and as changes take root, the Chartered Institute, through its examiners, may wish to test your knowledge and awareness of these changes and their implications with regard to marketing practice. For example, in the public sector, increasing attention is being paid to the marketing of services and the application of marketing principles and practice to the non-profit making and public sectors. Thus, you can now expect to see these areas forming a wider focus for the mini-case examinations.

3.1 Summary of learning points

1   The Chartered Institute of Marketing's mini cases are specifically designed to test your skills in application rather than your ability to write academic type essays.

2   As in business, effective time allocation is essential. The proportion of total marks accounted for by each question provides a clue as to what this should be. Where no indication is given it is reasonably safe to assume that all questions are accorded equal marks.

3   Beware of making your analysis of the mini case your full answer unless, of course, the questions specifically ask you to do this.

4   Do not waste time on extended general introductions which are designed merely to analyse the existing position; this will only waste valuable time and not earn marks. It is so easy to overrun time when answering the mini-case questions.

5   Ensure that you adopt the correct format for your answers. Normally, this will be report or memo-type format.

4

TACKLING MINI CASES

4.1 An overall framework

We have seen that one of the key differences between the mini cases and
the extended analysis and decision case is the fact that the mini case is
unseen, so the first time you will see the mini case for each of the three
subjects in which this format is used will be in the examination itself. A
further key difference which we have seen, and which also has an
important bearing on how you tackle the mini case, is the fact that you are
given the questions at the same time as the case. The final key difference
for tackling the mini case is that you have *only 1½ hours* to complete the
task.

Bearing these differences in mind, here is a suggested framework for
dealing with the mini case.

```
┌─────────────────────────┐
│   Familiarization with  │
│   case and questions    │
└────────────┬────────────┘
┌────────────┴────────────┐
│       Analysis of       │
│       questions/        │
│      instructions       │
└────────────┬────────────┘
┌────────────┴────────────┐
│     Analysis of case    │
│    material in relation  │
│     to questions set    │
└────────────┬────────────┘
┌────────────┴────────────┐
│      Preparation of     │
│   answers to questions  │
│    using appropriate    │
│          format         │
└─────────────────────────┘
```

4.2 Using this format

4.2.1 *Stage 1: Familiarization with case and questions*

Read through the case and questions quickly a couple of times to familiarize yourself with the case and question scenario. At this stage you should avoid the strong temptation to start writing answers or suggesting detailed solutions to the problems which you spot. At this stage you are simply getting the 'feel' of what the situation and company is 'about', set against the context of the questions/ requirements posed by the examiner.

4.2.2 *Stage 2: Analysis of questions/instructions*

Now turn your attention to the specific questions/instructions which will accompany the mini cases. It is most important that you follow these to the letter. It may appear strange to have to stress this obvious point but as we shall see it is still a major point of criticism of candidates by the examiners. For example, if the question asks you to advise on a promotional plan do not subsequently advise on a plan for the marketing mix.

In particular at this stage you should note any instructions as to the *role* you are to assume. For example:

Are you to be a member of the organization?

If so, in what capacity?

Alternatively, for example, you might be asked to assume the role of outside adviser/consultant to the company in the case.

Whatever the role, you should be careful to assume the appropriate stance.

- In analysing the questions/instructions you should carefully note the mark allocation for each section which should guide you as to the relative importance, and therefore the amount of time, you should devote to each part of your answer.

4.2.3 *Stage 3: Analysis of case material in relation to questions set*

Now, and only now, are you in a position to work through the case material in detail. Bearing in mind the tasks set for you by the examiner, you should work through the case noting and writing down your *general observations* and any *salient* facts and figures.

Remember, this is your analysis in preparing for your answers, *not the answers themselves*. You should, therefore, prepare this outline in rough and cross it out afterwards. In other words, unless specifically required to do so do not include it as part of your answers. It is for your purposes, not the examiner's.

Again, because of the differences between the mini cases and the maxi case of Analysis and Decision, it is unlikely that you will be required, or able to prepare say a *detailed* SWOT analysis or a *full* marketing audit. However, so far as it is possible, there is nothing wrong with using these in the context of *analysing* a mini case, so long as you do not simply rewrite the case under these headings. Overall, your observations of facts and issues should be concise and tailored to the questions themselves.

4.2.4 *Stage 4: Preparation of specific answers to questions set*

You should now be in a position to turn your attention to producing specific answers to the questions set. Clearly, the content of your answers will need to reflect the particular questions on each case, but remember that the mini cases are designed to test your *application skills*. You will, therefore, need to select from your acquired knowledge those techniques, concepts and skills which are appropriate to the questions asked.

In preparing your answers you should bear these points in mind:

- *Avoid 'waffle' and extended general introductions.*
  Remember, you have little time to answer the questions set. More importantly, there are *no marks* for general situation analyses or for observations *not directly related to the questions*. In particular, do not waste valuable time by writing down the questions again.
- *Note carefully any constraints and time scales.*
  One of the most frequent criticisms aimed at mini-case answers by the senior examiners is that the candidate has come up with impractical suggestions. As we have noted, very often the mini cases deal with the marketing problems of smaller or inexperienced companies. A company with an annual turnover of, say, £½ million is unlikely to be able to afford, for example, a national television advertising campaign or, say, an extensive and expensive programme of international marketing research. The recognition of the limiting effects of such resource constraints – financial, human and organizational – and a reflection of these in your answers is yet another variation on the test of your ability to practise marketing. Sometimes the cases themselves will contain specific information on budgets, e.g. for promotion. Do not exceed them; demonstrate your professional knowledge of current costs and practice.
  In this context note, too, any indications of time scales in a mini case. For example, if the case indicates or specifies a plan of action to cover the next twelve months, make sure that your plan covers *precisely* this period, not the next three months or the next five years. Where a series

of actions is required over the requisite period, your answer should demonstrate clearly the timing and sequence of these actions over the specified time period.

- *Clearly state any assumptions you have made.*
  Often in case studies you will need to make assumptions and in this respect the mini cases are no different. The examiners will be happy to accept any assumption *so long as it is reasonable in the context of the case.* You should clearly specify *any* assumptions you have made in arriving at your proposals for courses of action. In fact, so long as your assumptions meet the 'reasonable' criterion, you can use your assumptions to your advantage. An example will serve to illustrate:

The following communications plan for the company is based on the following assumptions:
- The annual rate of overall market growth will continue at 3 per cent per annum for the next three years.
- All new products are produced to BS 5270.
- Potential new competitors will find it difficult to enter the market quickly.

Used wisely and creatively, assumptions can help you to clear away any considerations which, though important, are peripheral to the particular aspects on which the questions centre. They can also be used to support the line of argument in your answers.

- *Suggest specific courses of action.*
  Again, in line with what the mini cases are intended to test, your answers should indicate *solutions to problems* through clearly specified courses of action rather than simply the identification of the problems themselves.

  In most questions, the action required will be explicit in the questions themselves. For example:

  'Write a brief for an export market research plan with the aim of identifying overseas target markets. . . .'

In some questions, alternative courses of action may be open to the company in the case: indeed, you may be asked to identify these. However, wherever possible and appropriate, you should be careful not to use a mere listing of alternatives as a means of avoiding a commitment to a particular alternative. At the very least you should prioritize your alternatives and give supporting reasons for your choice.

- *Do not over-complicate your answers.*
  Essentially the mini cases are not over-complicated. They are testing your ability to *apply* key concepts and techniques from each of the final year Diploma subject areas. Keep your answers brief, to the point and

in the format specified. Above all, do not over-complicate your answers.

To summarize some of the most important considerations in actually tackling a mini case, here are the key points to remember when preparing your answers:

- Avoid 'waffle' and extended general introductions.
- Note constraints and time scales.
- State assumptions.
- Propose relevant action.
- Do not over-complicate.
- Answer the actual questions set.

Just in case these points seem rather obvious, let us now have a look at another example of a previous mini case, this time that set for the June 1986 planning and control paper, together with the published examiners' comments on the assessed examination scripts. Where appropriate, both case and comments are annotated to underline some of the points already made.

Note: In order to get maximum value for this second mini-case example, you should read through the case and questions themselves at least twice before turning to the examiner's report.

Diploma in Marketing

MARKETING MANAGEMENT – PLANNING AND CONTROL

Time: 14.00–17.00   Friday, 13th June, 1986
3 hours duration

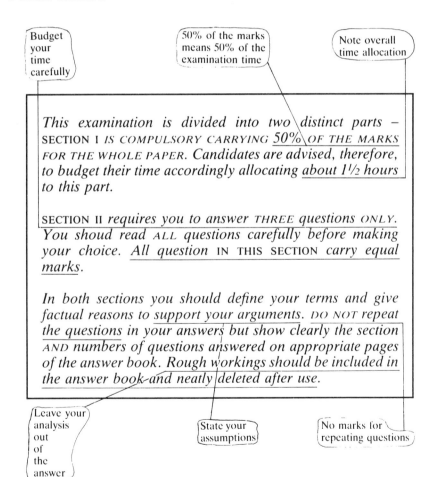

Budget your time carefully

50% of the marks means 50% of the examination time

Note overall time allocation

This examination is divided into two distinct parts – SECTION I *IS COMPULSORY CARRYING* 50% *OF THE MARKS FOR THE WHOLE PAPER. Candidates are advised, therefore, to budget their time accordingly allocating about 1½ hours to this part.*

SECTION II *requires you to answer* THREE *questions* ONLY. *You shoud read* ALL *questions carefully before making your choice. All question* IN THIS SECTION *carry equal marks.*

In both sections you should define your terms and give factual reasons to support your arguments. DO NOT *repeat the questions in your answers but show clearly the section* AND *numbers of questions answered on appropriate pages of the answer book. Rough workings should be included in the answer book and neatly deleted after use.*

Leave your analysis out of the answer

State your assumptions

No marks for repeating questions

Mini Cases in Marketing

The copyright of all Institute of Marketing examination material is held by the Institute.

No case study or question may be reproduced without its prior permission, which must be obtained in writing.

MARKETING MANAGEMENT – PLANNING AND CONTROL
Approximate time: 1½ hours   June 1986

Section I

Olworth Leisure Centre

There are several hundred leisure/sports/recreation centres in the UK jointly provided by public authorities and local education authorities.

A typical centre includes a sports hall, a swimming pool, two gymnasia, squash courts, sauna, solarium, lounge bar, games area and is located in a surrounding fielded area for track sports and athletics. The indoor sports hall would be marked out for badminton, netball, volley ball, etc. and might be large enough for an occasional indoor tennis court.

Olworth is a population centre of about 10,000 inhabitants and considered to be an area of high deprivation and isolation, resulting in relatively high rates of crime and vandalism. Most of the menfolk work in nearby coalmines on a shift system.

The district council responsible for Olworth are considering building a leisure centre in the conurbation for use by its local population, but with the hope of attracting people from surrounding villages and hamlets within a radius of 10 miles with an additional population of 12,000. Due to financial and other constraints building is likely to take place in three phases over a total of three years.

Obviously objectives for the provision and use of leisure centre services are not necessarily based upon profit as such, although a level of income contributing considerably towards running costs is projected.

Leisure centre services are not always in a situation of economic balance where demand matches supply and it is not unusual for some activities/facilities to be overbooked, e.g. squash and swimming, whilst other minority sports facilities are grossly under-utilised. A major problem facing local authority-provided centres has been the maximization of usage during weekdays. In the evenings and weekends, with the demand from the general public and various clubs and organizations, the space more than sells itself.

Olworth Council see this project somewhat as a marketing planning and control exercise. They are anxious to achieve a good match between supply and demand and are aware of the importance of the four Ps (place being in the sense of timing of a given leisure facility and its duration as well as location) in this aim. They have asked a local college to put this project to their Diploma in Marketing course members in the hope of obtaining some practical help in the form of a marketing plan. As a <u>member of this course</u> your individual task is to:

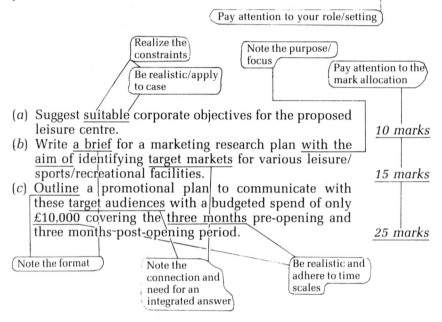

(a) Suggest <u>suitable</u> corporate objectives for the proposed leisure centre.   *10 marks*

(b) Write <u>a brief</u> for a marketing research plan <u>with the</u> <u>aim of</u> identifying <u>target markets</u> for various leisure/ sports/recreational facilities.   *15 marks*

(c) <u>Outline</u> a promotional plan to communicate with these <u>target audiences</u> with a budgeted spend of only £10,000 covering the three months pre-opening and three months-post-opening period.   *25 marks*

Analysis of the examiner's report

Again, many of the points which have been highlighted seem rather obvious. With this in mind, however, now let us have a look at the examiner's report.

Planning and control – examiner's report

June 1986

General comments

Overall, more candidates are demonstrating adequacy in the professionalism of their answers and general approach. Very few candidates unnecessarily repeated questions before answering. Failures tend to show marked weaknesses in one section of the paper rather than both. A good proportion of examinees demonstrating an adequate knowledge of the syllabus in Section II were found wanting in their ability to apply this knowledge to the practical case situation. Often students who were clearly lacking in sufficient knowledge to gain passes in Section II did somewhat better in the practical case situation.

> Clearly, they have been repeated in the past

> Poor time allocation

> note the emphasis

Failures also showed a tendency to 'waffle'; that is to avoid directly addressing the question, spending at least the first page of their answers on general introductions. Many students did SWOT or situational analyses or introductions to Section I. Candidates are urged to recognize that examiners are looking for points relevant to the question in order to award marks and that scene-setting gains them few, if any, marks and is essentially wasting valuable time. Equally students, in making a valid point, should avoid subsequent over elaboration of that single point over the next page or more before making the next valid point. This often leads to answers four pages or more long containing only four valid points out of the 10 the examiner is looking for. Such an approach, apart from failing to gain sufficient marks to pass quantitatively, also demonstrates a failure to plan answers, which is depressing in a subject testing planning and control.

A disappointing number of examinees failed to adopt report format in answering Section I. Essay format was completely inappropriate for stating corporate objectives, for presenting a marketing brief and even more so for an *outline* promotional *plan*.

> Lack of ability to apply

> note the need for balance!

> Avoid extended general introductions

> Analysis and general introduction, not answers

> Make what you write score marks

> Substance scores points

> Plan your work and work your plan

> Wrong format

Incredibly, some candidates used essay form for the
checklist called for in Section II, Question 1.

Wrong format

Adopt report style

Some failure to understand what is meant by terms
such as a brief, marketing mix, promotion mix, test
marketing, corporate, etc. was apparent. When given
a choice, candidates should avoid answering questions using terms they do not properly understand as
such basic mistakes tend to deflate the mark the
examiners can properly award.

It is hoped that future examinees reading this
report will also read other examiners' reports which
contain valuable points on what to avoid in their
endeavours to pass the examination in this subject
and that they will also avail themselves of the opportunity to acquire specimen answers to previous
papers so as to make themselves aware of the content
and standard of answers ideally required as well as
of the approach looked for in answering particular
types of questions.

A tip for exam preparation

Section I (mini-case)

Know your subject

In answering question (*a*) many candidates showed
themselves unable to distinguish between objectives,
strategies and tactics. Others adopted a functional
rather than corporate approach. Some candidates
gave just one objective (ignoring the question's
request for objectives) and some gave a long list of
trivialities, the record being 23!

Ignoring the question

The main cause of failure for question (*b*) was a
lack of understanding of how to write a brief in the
first place and, secondly, ignorance of the content of
marketing research plans. Many candidates failed
to consider that valuable information could be
obtained in the form of secondary data, especially by
looking at the nature and success of other leisure
centres in similar areas. A depressing number of
candidates suggested acquiring primary data on just
about everything but crucial facts such as how many
respondents would visit the centre, to use which
particular facilities, at what frequencies, based on
what price expectations and what media would
reach them effectively. Briefs should of course
allude to timing and cost considerations.

Relevance

Remember time scales

Consider scale of operation and cost constraints

Answers to question (c) were on the whole well done with most candidates sketching in costed media schedules split into pre- and post-opening activities. There were also some good creative ideas, particularly from overseas candidates, who suggested PA vehicles touring streets, audio-visual presentations to clubs, etc. Whilst the approaching of regional TV for free publicity on the grounds of news value was acceptable, the idea that this would provide *continuous* coverage was untenable. Unfortunately, too many candidates from overseas suggested paid-for TV advertising at ridiculously low costs, failing to realise that the budget would not permit such an expensive promotional activity and that *regional* TV would not in any case be cost effective for a *local* sports centre, neither would *national* sports/leisure magazine advertising. Too many candidates also omitted any check on promotional expenditure effectiveness in their outline plans.

Failure to note contstraints

Lack of realism

Lack of professionalism

You will no doubt note from the examiners' comments that failure to spot and/or take account of the seemingly 'obvious' points underpin many of the criticisms. You can also see the importance of adopting a practical/ professional rather than academic approach. For example, note the frequent comments as to budgeting, costing and timing, all of which would be important if you were actually in a business situation.

To summarize, you should now be quite clear about the format of mini cases; what is expected of you in the examination; the key skills required; the overall approach to tackling the mini case; and the pitfalls to avoid.

There now follows two more Chartered Institute of Marketing diploma mini cases (international and communications) together with the senior examiner's comments for each of these subjects. Again, we have highlighted certain comments that have been made.

INTERNATIONAL ASPECTS

Approx. time: 1½ hours   June 1986

Section I

The MacHamish Distillery

As he looked down the winding road in the remote Highland glen where his family had been distilling whisky for several generations, Angus MacHamish sampled the latest batch. 'Well up to standard,' he said 'In five years it will be reasonable, and then in ten we can bottle and market it. I wonder if we ought to increase the quantity in the next few batches?' His father, recently retired from the business, was more inclined to be cautious. 'All the big distilleries have had their fingers burned with the fall in sales since 1979 – nearly 20 per cent down since then. Everyone overproduced and is overstocked by two years' requirements, and production is cut to half what it was.' 'But that is for the standard, blended grain whiskies – premium brands like ours have maintained their sales and even increased them over that time,' said Angus.

Whisky is produced from cereals, which are fermented and then distilled. The cereals used vary with the type of whisky required. Bourbon and rye, produced in the USA, must contain at least 15 per cent of maize and 51 per cent of rye respectively in their cereal content, while the true Scotch whisky is produced from two main bases – malt, which is made from malted barley only, with no additional cereals, and is twice distilled by a batch process; and grain whisky, which is distilled in a continuous process from a mixture of malted and unmalted barley and other grains, usually maize. Arising from this, and apart from a very small quantity of pure grain whisky, three types of Scotch are normally produced for consumption:

1 A single malt whisky – from one distillery only.
2 A blended malt whisky – malts from several distilleries.
3 Blended Scotch whiskies – blends of malt and grain whiskies.

The malts accounted for only 2 per cent of the sales volume; the other 98 per cent of the 251 million litres produced in 1983 being blended.

These are further subdivided into:

(*a*) De luxe premium brands (75% proof) – 3%
(*b*) Standard brands (70% proof) – 80%
(*c*) Own label and cheap brands (65% proof)– 15%

The production and blending of different whiskies to give desirable and consistent products is an art learned only by experience, for whiskies made even by the same method and from the same raw materials in two different distilleries will be unlikely to taste the same. So far it has proved difficult to equal the quality of Scotch whisky anywhere else in the world, although Japan has been striving hard.

The decline in the blended Scotch whisky sales can be ascribed to several causes common over much of the world – the economic recession and heavy duties payable were significant, but even more the ageing profile of whisky drinkers. Over one-third of buyers were in the 45 to 64 age group, and the younger drinkers preferred gins and vodkas, or lighter drinks, to whiskies.

Exports too had declined in volume by 9 per cent between 1977 and 1983; the EEC countries were the largest market in terms of value, taking some £230m out of a total export value of £864m; and the USA was the largest market (30 per cent) by volume. This was followed by Japan, in second place by volume of sales; and to lesser degrees by France, West Germany, Spain and Canada.

As might be expected with such individualistic products and fragmented markets, branding was very important. The total of advertising expenditure by whisky firms was some £10m in 1984 – the seven largest distilleries spent some £6m. Below-the-line promotions, such as the sponsorship of sports events, were also widely used. One-third of all UK sales were made through public houses and hotels; of the remaining two-thirds over half of all sales were now made through grocers and supermarkets, and over a third through off licences and wine merchants; while other outlets included a significant proportion, usually of the premium brands, through duty free shops at ports. The MacHamish distillery spent some £75,000 on limited press advertising, as all his sales were through high class wine merchants in the UK only.

Unlike his father, Angus wished to build on the established strength of MacHamish, and in view of the static situation in the UK, wanted to consider overseas markets. While some stock could be immediately available, any significant increase in sales would be a long-term operation, allowing plenty of time to develop the operation. He would now require advice.

The questions below draw attention to some international aspects of the situation, *all* of which you are required to answer. There are other aspects relevant to the possible development of the firm's activities which you may wish to consider, and credit will be given for suitable observations.

Questions

Advise MacHamish on:

(*a*) A suitable procedure to find possible markets overseas for
their whisky. (30%)
(*b*) An outline plan for selecting appropriate distribution
channels. (30%)
(*c*) Promotional activities. (30%)

Additional observations and presentation (10%)

100%

Analysis of the examiner's report

International Aspects – examiner's report

June 1986

General comments

As in most examinations, particular questions are set
and worded in such a way as to not only test the
student's knowledge of the relevant area and his or
her ability to apply that knowledge in given circumstances, but also to be able to do so in managerial,
decision making fashion. To this end, the questions
in both parts 1 and 2 are so phrased as to require
some definite approach or framework in the answer.
Considerable latitude is given in the actual contents
as long as they are appropriate, but at the end of the
question or part, the examiner has to ask himself
whether or not the student has actually answered the
question as set. All too frequently a particular word
or phrase is noted, but then the actual question is
mentally rephrased or rewritten by the student, who
thereby misses the actual points required. However
correct the contents of such work may be, few marks
can be given if the actual question is not answered.

Note the examiner's objectives

Clear thinking, clear logic are needed

Report format is essential

Note, there are no 'right' answers in case work

The key reason for failure

An alternative, but equally fatal approach, is for the student to seize upon a particular word or phrase and then to write anything and everything about it, irrespective of the relevance or application. In this area, an improvement has been noted, however, that there are fewer examples of complete checklists being regurgitated without consideration of the relevance of individual items, and this does indicate an improvement in the application of the managerial approach.

Note the examiner's objectives

Section 1 (mini case)

The MacHamish Distillery

The need to read and understand the questions carefully before answering is particularly relevant to at least the first two questions in the mini case. Surely it should not be necessary to state what is meant by a 'procedure' and a 'plan'? But the number of students who completely ignored any sequence or direction in the methods to be used, let alone the steps or actions which would be dependent on a previous activity, cost many their pass marks. Similarly, a plan of any kind is an outline of actions proposed, again sequential, which would lead from some defined objective to some control to ensure a successful operation. In too many cases, these approaches were just not followed. Where a 'procedure' was outlined, all too often the result was a full market research across the whole world, eliminating some countries for one reason, then a second batch for another, until by dint of much hard work, time and certainly far more money than MacHamish would ever have been able to spend, the one or two countries for the first attack were produced. This type of answer is not wrong – it is usually too generalized to be so – but it is not all that realistic for a firm of MacHamish's indicated size and resources, let alone the unique product itself and the limited and specialized potential market for it.

Virtually no useful references were made to two particularly limiting parameters: that of the ten year production period and the actual quantities available either for immediate sale or at particular periods in

Read these before you start reading the mini case to help to focus your thoughts

Have a planning structure prepared that you can use if requested

Consider the cost implications of your recommendations. Remember to balance the scale of your suggestions with the financial constraints of the organization

Realism must prevail

Identify the constraints which limit the company's market potential

the future. No actual figures were given – or necessary – but a reference to the consideration of the stock figures and future availability over the next ten years would have been the basis for the answers to all three parts of the question, to give some element of realism to the actual distribution channels or the promotions selected.

The misreading of the question continued to be a major cause of low marks in part (*b*). A plan was required to enable a selection to be made of the most appropriate distribution channel(s). There could have been several quite reasonable distribution methods possible and acceptable; but what was *not* required was a complete list of all possible export methods (including local production overseas, either directly or under licence!) without any attempt to discriminate and choose between them; and presented as a list without any indication of a selection procedure. How to organize the selection procedure was the requirement here, not just the range of choices possible.

Another classic error

For part (*c*) 'promotional activities' were left wide open for any appropriate treatment. Unfortunately far too many students were content with repeating broadly the methods already mentioned in the study without any evaluation or development. Few attempted, for instance, to quantify, however crudely, the funds available or needed for the overseas operation, let alone to consider what the actual tasks and objectives of the promotion were to be. In this, too, a consideration of the particular channel characteristics would have been appropriate.

Be clear on the purpose and the means of achieving it

Justify your approach. Show the rationale for your recommendation

As a final observation, all three parts should relate to each other to form a coherent whole; the promotional activities should have been evaluated and appropriate for use as part of the distribution selection process, and this again should have been related to the market selection cases.

As a postscript, the senior examiner is still trying to work out what would be involved in the case of one answer received, which recommended that MacHamish should emphasize the provision of 'a full after sales service, including the provision of spare parts'! Presumably, for legless drinkers?

MARKETING COMMUNICATIONS

Approximate time: 1½ hours   June 1986

Section I

Enigma Travel Co. Ltd

A Background

- In the winter 1983–84 and summer 1984 seasons, industry figures show that UK holidaymakers took 9 million inclusive tours abroad.
- Of these, 5.8 million (64 per cent) were booked through travel agents.
- The top six operators (companies A, B, C, D, E and F) accounted for some 52 per cent of the business through travel agents and 33 per cent of the total inclusive tour market.
- All of these operators offered very much the same 'product' and, with the exception of company C, all advertised their 'brands' in the media.
- In 1983–84 media expenditure on foreign tours and holidays was £32.5m compared to £36m in the same period for 1982–83.
- In addition to media expenditure, companies A, B, C and D all put money 'below-the-line' by offering incentives to travel agents. No figures are available for this expenditure.
- The number of travel agency retail outlets in the UK is some 5300. This consists of four defined types:

  (*a*) Single outlets.
  (*b*) Small chains (2 to 5 shops).
  (*c*) Medium-sized chains (6 to 19 shops).
  (*d*) Large chains (20+ shops).

B Problem

The end of 1984 had seen heavy price cutting and a tendency for the consumer to book much later. January no longer appeared to be the peak booking month. These two trends looked like continuing into 1985 and the industry was becoming increasingly competitive.

The products in the marketplace all appeared to be broadly the same and all operators had trimmed profit margins to increase the competitive edge. Nevertheless, because of better buying power the larger operators were able to get better hotel rates and thus appeared more price competitive. This buying power seemed to increase proportionately with the number of passengers the operator carried.

Operator E (Enigma Travel) trades under four separate brand names, which have been acquired or developed over the years. Individual brochures are produced for each product and separate advertising has been undertaken for each brand.

Steven Gold is Sales Marketing Director of company E. He has a sales-force of some ten representatives, smaller than that of his competitors. Sales to UK holidaymakers are through travel agents, although Enigma Travel does have regional offices in Glasgow, Newcastle, Manchester and Birmingham as well as the head office in London.

Steven Gold has seen his sales gradually decreasing over the past few years and the crunch has now come. His parent company require him to increase his share of the inclusive tours market by 3 per cent in 1984–85. He has been given a budget of £2m over the next year to do this.

Steven has a month to prepare his communication plan for presentation to the main board.

(*a*) List the factors he should take into account when preparing
  his plan, explaining briefly why these factors are important. *15 marks*
(*b*) Prepare an outline marketing communication plan placing
  special emphasis on the sales end of the business. *35 marks*

Analysis of the examiner's report

Marketing communications – examiner's report

June 1986

General comments

Candidates should:

> A clear directive from the examiner

1 Answer the questions set, in the format required.
2 Do so in the logical business-like manner expected
  of any marketing practitioner.
3 Do so legibly.

The examiners were distressed by the large number of candidates who had clearly worked hard and

acquired considerable knowledge but who, rather
than answer the questions set, paraded all they knew
about the topic in question or simply rewrote the
mini case. This is a waste of candidates' time, just as
much as the examiners'.

> You must
> answer the
> questions set
> or run the
> risk of certain
> failure

> No marks are
> given for the
> regurgitation
> of case material

No doubt similar comments apply to other diploma
subjects and similar remarks are made year after
year. The comments were alas particularly applicable
to the June 1986 examination entries.

Section 1 (mini case)

In dealing with the mini case, candidates should
realize the importance of marketing analysis and
grasp the sequential nature of marketing communications planning and strategy. The need for a
'planning' approach does not, however, mean filling
answer books with pages of marketing audits and
situation or SWOT analyses: these are simply techniques candidates can (and should) use in getting to
grips with the problems posed. The techniques are
not answers in themselves: they are an aid to thought
and not a substitute for it.

> Use these
> techniques
> *only* when
> asked – otherwise
> you waste valuable
> mark-earning time

The Enigma Travel case was not complicated, but
many candidates made it unnecessarily so. It is
about a marketing executive whose company faces
difficult conditions: he has been given a target and a
budget by his parent company and has a month to
prepare an outline communications plan – within
the restraints of the budget – to achieve that target.
Against this scenario, the examination posed candidates two specific tasks:

> The emphasis
> is upon
> professional
> practice, not
> theory

(a) List the factors the executive should take into
    account when preparing his plan, explaining
    why they are important. The executive was *not*
    required to propose action at this point, but
    simply to list those factors he should consider
    before making plans, with reasons why these
    factors should be considered. The factors are
    many, and would include Enigma's four brands
    and four regional offices, the public tendency to
    book late and follow competitive pricing, with
    64 per cent of bookings coming through 5300
    travel agency retail outlets of four defined types

> Structure the
> content of
> your answer
> according to
> the precise
> instructions
> given in the
> question

and most tour operators offering below-the-line incentives.

(b) Prepare an outline marketing communications plan, placing special emphasis on the sales end of the business.

Many candidates restricted themselves to advertising proposals <u>rather than give a full marketing communications plan</u>, while others ignored the required emphasis on the sales end. Some even gave no indication of how they would spend £2m – how could they expect the examiners, let alone the parent company, to approve their outline proposals?

Answer the questions set

We now put these lessons into practice by working through a sample mini case and answer for each of the diploma subjects. Each of the sample cases is from, or is typical, of recent Chartered Institute of Marketing examinations.

5

WORKED EXAMPLES OF MINI CASES

In order to help you to learn from these worked examples, for each case we have included the thought process, analysis and note making which a candidate would need to go through in preparing answers. Each specimen case, therefore, has been examined from the perspective of an actual candidate faced with the case in an examination. As well as answers, there are also pointers to how the candidate should have approached the cases following the basic framework, which we established earlier. These are *for your guidance only and would not normally be included in analysing and answering an examination case.*

You should also note that the specimen answers which accompany the cases, both in this and the next section, are for your guidance and should not be considered as 'perfect' solutions. In the world of marketing there is never just one correct answer.

We shall start by examining a sample mini case on the international aspects of marketing paper, working through it in some considerable detail. This is followed by a second sample case, this time on marketing communications, which summarizes the approach that a good candidate would have taken in preparing his or her answers. This second case also illustrates a slightly different, but equally acceptable approach to structuring the format of your answers.

Finally, a third sample case is from the marketing management – planning and control syllabus. By the time you reach this third case you should be getting the feel of how to approach the mini cases. Therefore for this final specimen case we have simply pointed to the major consideration in arriving at a set of solutions to the problems posed in the case.

INTERNATIONAL ASPECTS OF MARKETING

Karlstein GmbH

Karlstein GmbH was formed some twenty years ago by a metal processing manufacturer based in Hanover, West Germany.

The company manufactures bathroom fixtures and fittings, principally for plumbing application (including taps, joints and shower fittings).

A wide range of end users exists, including domestic householders and industrial/institutional buyers.

In the last year the company achieved market shares of 36% in West Germany; 10% in France and 3% in Belgium. In addition, 5% of total production was shipped to a major wholesaler in Miami, USA. Total turnover exceeds 40 million DM.

The wide range of fittings varies in size, style, colour, metal and plastic finishings to occupy bottom and top end market positions.

A feasibility study has recently been completed to assess the potential of the UK market. Encouraging results have now stimulated the company to pursue actively the UK market with a target date for entry in ten months time.

Questions

1 Advise the company of the options open to achieve UK market entry.
2 Outline the potential 'difficulties' involved with each option.
3 Select and justify a method of market entry and give a detailed account of the physical distribution implications.

Guidance notes on sample mini case 1

1 *Familiarization with case and questions*

Note: The case chosen here for analysis is deliberately short as this is the first one. Cases are progressively longer as we proceed through the text.

1.1 Before you write anything, you should first read through the case and questions *at least twice*. A good tip is to read the questions asked before you read the case. By so doing, you will read the case with some idea of the issues that you will have to address.

1.2 Having acquainted yourself with the content of the case and the questions, read through the case slowly, underlining or highlighting the key issues and salient facts. At this stage, you should confine yourself to general but succinct observations, not extended general observations.

Here are some examples from the case:

- Twenty-year-old West German manufacturer.
- Products manufactured: bathroom fixtures and fittings in metal and plastic finishes.
- Markets served: domestic householders; industrial and institutional buyers.
- Wide range of fittings in different sizes, styles and colours to suit as wide a proportion of the market as possible.
- Market shares:

	%
West Germany =	36
France =	10
Belgium =	3
USA (Miami) =	5
	54 Remainder = 46%

- Total turnover = 40 million DM plus.
  Turnover to markets stated must be in the order of 25 million or so DM.
- Decision has been taken to enter the UK market with target entry date in ten months time.

Note: You do not need to write down these facts and observations as this would waste examination time. It is sufficient that you merely underline them where appropriate or use a highlighting pen.

2 Analysis of questions/instructions

You should now read through the instructions and questions again very carefully. In this sample case you should have noted the following:

2.1 The number of questions together with the mark, and therefore time allocation for each (here, three questions with marks not ascribed, so it is fair to assume that each will be marked $33\frac{1}{3}\%$). This means that the time to be allocated is half an hour on each question, minus the time spent reading through and understanding the case.

In many mini cases unequal marks are awarded to individual questions, and in such cases it is advisable to allocate time in accordance with the ratio of marks to be given to each individual question.

As a guide, you should allocate your time like this:

Time allowed for mini case = 90 minutes
Less preparation/reading time = 15 minutes
Time available for writing answers = 75 minutes

2.2 All questions are specific and need to have a structured answer in the form of observations and/or recommendations:

- Methods of UK market entry.
- Difficulties involved with each option.
- Select and justify one method from those cited and detail physical distribution implications.

  Note: Sometimes there is an additional open ended question that gives a small number of marks for additional observations.

2.3 You are not given a specific role to play in the company other than that of adviser/consultant.

2.4 Any information/instructions as to timing, budgets, constraints, etc. in the questioning should be noted and adhered to. In this case such information is not added, but sometimes a constraint like a 'limited budget' is referred to.

2.5 Any information or instructions as to format should be noted. No specific reference is made to this in this particular case, so you should adopt report style format. Report format is the usual style to adopt, so ensure that you are fully versed in your 'favourite' report style before the examination.

3 Analysis of case material in relation to the questions

It was mentioned earlier that now, and only now, is the candidate in a position to work through the case material in detail. You should now be fully familiar with the case, the questions and your role. You can now proceed to analyse the case in the context of the questions asked.

Mini cases, as the title implies, contain only limited information and consequently the amount of analysis that you can undertake is limited. In the context of the specimen case and questions under review, here are some of the key elements that you should consider:

3.1 You have the total sales turnover (40 million plus DM. You have the market shares for certain countries. It is safe to assume, initially at least, that total sales are not going to be higher than one of these established markets. This means that sales are likely to be less than 3 million DM.

3.2 The immediate problem is how to attain market entry into the United Kingdom successfully. This will be at a cost in terms of logistics, promotion, etc.

3.3 The company is experienced in marketing in non-West German markets (only 36 per cent of sales are made in West Germany).

3.4 Recommendations as to developing the United Kingdom market will need to reflect assumptions as to the problems associated with each method of distribution within the context of the material to be marketed.

Note on the analysis

This is the kind of analysis and thought processes that you should have gone through in preparing to answer the questions on the Karlstein mini case. You should also note that in illustrating the analysis, we have necessarily made more detailed and expansive notes than would be possible or necessary in the examination itself.

In the examination paper you would simply be preparing rough notes and pointers in your analysis (normally at the head of the paper in rough pencil notes – deleted after you have completed the answer). Remember that the examiner is interested only in your answers to the specific questions and not in the rough notes on your analysis. Doing it in this manner is useful, because quite often when you are writing the answer, further thoughts might occur to you. Such thoughts can then be added to the rough notes to be included in the appropriate part of your narrative. Quite often, too, thoughts occur to you afterwards. Although it might not look aesthetically pleasing, the best course to adopt here is to ensure that you leave sufficient space between points so it is possible to insert the forgotten point afterwards without 'crowding' the appearance of your paper too much. Otherwise, leave sufficient space between individual parts of your answer and put an asterisk at the place where you wish to insert the extra information (with an appropriate note to the examiner, e.g. 'Please see additional point at the end of this section for insertion here').

4 Preparation of answers

The following is a suggested solution of the Karlstein mini case illustrating the way in which you might have set about answering the specific questions. First, simply read through the answer shown, remembering of course that this represents only a sample of a variety of possible ways of resolving the issues under review.

International aspects of marketing

Karlstein GmbH – suggested solution

General observations

1 The company has a significant market position in Europe; an apparent market strength to operate on.
2 It has substantial international experience.
3 The product has a wide range of applications; they are not specialists. The product is a general type.
4 Therefore, it is a multiproduct company. Also they have brand recognition through establishment within the market.
5 The management is shrewd and forward thinking because of the feasibility study.
6 The *stimulus* that is driving the situation is that the company is expanding and that there is planned growth.
7 A planned international organization is taking place with determination to penetrate the UK market.

Question

1 *Options*:
  (*a*) Direct export.
  (*b*) To set up a manufacturing base in the UK.
  (*c*) The appointment of sales distribution.
  (*d*) Joint venture with existing UK company with established distribution channel.
  (*e*) To manufacture under licence.
  (*f*) To set up own sales industry.
  (*g*) To set up a pioneering sales force to test market the product.
  (*h*) *Acquisition   forward integration*: (distributor and wholesaler with existing sales force)
  horizontal integration: (a UK-based manufacturer perhaps 51 per cent only to buy the controlling interest) – it may be less than 50 per cent – we only need the percentage that can control.

International problems:
The time it takes to:
• get recognized
• obtain distribution
• obtain market position

Acquisition or mergers are only good for well-established companies. They are not good for young blood.

2 *Difficulties of each option*:

(*a*) *direct exporting*
- market acceptance
- market resistance to a foreign brand name
- time to get distribution penetration
- control (little control on growth)
- little trade penetration into the product and end-user application
- delays in payment

(*b*) *New manufacturing base*
- investment
- location
- training of workforce
- employment of qualified staff
- obtaining the correct advice (on location of base and benefits of different choices)
- time delay to obtain market acceptance, trade acceptance
- overall risks of new venture

(*c*) *Sales distribution of agents*
- difficult to get good agents (biggest may not be best)
- the on-cost of appointing the agents has to be passed on to the final price to the consumer
- the agent may find difficulty in getting the product accepted (further market resistance)
- the performance of overtime may vary
- communication can be fragmented
- maintenance of sales effort
- problem of motivation
- the loyalty to the company is based purely on financial return
- agents may sell competing products

(*d*) *Joint venture*
- difficult to establish mutual commitment and understanding
- finding the right partner
- problems that arise after the joint venture is sealed, e.g. politics, power fight
- the need to achieve common objectives through a common interest
- the need to establish bases for profit repatriation and result contribution

(*e*) *Licensing*
- the appropriateness with reference to the market
- maintenance and achievement of standards
- the need to determine the real cost effectiveness
- loss of control

- the reputation of the product is at stake
- marketing is in the hands of a third party
- it is inappropriate for a multiproduct company with highly technical specification required
- it may conflict with the object of the licensor
- tax disadvantages with reference to royalties that must be paid
- the requirement of self-franchise over the licence and the link limits to growth potential

(f) *Sales subsidiary abroad* (quite a sensible option)
- investment
- time lag (in getting to understand the market, building the sales system and sales base)
- correct staffing
- need for pioneering
- the level of financial risk and meeting the objectives specified by the German company

(g) *Pioneering sales force or export sales force*
- need to integrate in a foreign country
- cultural differences
- gaining personal level acceptance
- to overcome the adjustment of the product to meet market requirements
- setting up a sales system
- maintaining motivation

(h) *Acquisition* (difficulties are short term)
- acquiring the right company
- securing investment rather than incurring additional cost
- getting the right acquisition profile

3 Suggested method of market entry is by *acquisition* and the reasons behind it are:
(a) Effective use of time in securing market penetration.
(b) Existing market position.
(c) Existing market contact.
(d) Existing sales system.
(e) Existing distribution channels.
(f) Knowledge of marketing institutions and facilities.
(g) Existing customer groupings.
(h) A ready-made company where the purchaser is buying years of investment in terms of corporate development.
(i) In short, it is a cost-effect method in gaining market entry and securing an established market position.

Physical distribution implications of the selected option
1 The need to standardize the paperwork system between the companies.

2 The need to set up an inventory system between the exporting and importing countries.
3 To ensure economical order quantities and delivery.
4 To use the most cost-effective method of distribution and yet maintain customer service levels.
5 To set a level for distribution form to meet the defined distribution objectives.
6 Road transportation (containerization using roll-on roll-off facilities for bulk orders) and rail transportation for smallest specialist orders.

The overall implication of the total distribution system is one of cost control.

Because the option has been selected the acquired company's distribution network will be fully utilised until such time as an alternative is required.

Notes on the answer

1 See how we have adopted the appropriate type of format for the answer.
2 It is made quite clear from the use of headings which questions are being addressed.
3 Any assumptions are clearly stated.
4 In order to put the case in the setting a 'general observations' section is included at the beginning. This does not necessarily score marks, but it does allow a smoother transition into the case analysis and it demonstrates that you, the candidate, have clear thought processes. More to the point, it might save time later in the analysis as you will not have to go into long explanations of why you are making such recommendations.
5 Where necessary and appropriate any detailed parts of the initial analysis can be included as a separate appendix (not necessary in this case).
6 Clear courses of action have been suggested within the constraints of the case scenario.

Undoubtedly, this answer would have scored high marks in an examination. Mini cases, however, often demand variations of this basic style. To illustrate this point we shall now examine in turn two further mini-case examples from the two other diploma examinations: marketing communications and marketing planning and control.

MARKETING COMMUNICATIONS
Approximate time: 1½ hours

United British Automobiles plc

In early February 1984 plans were well advanced for the production of a new range of mass market cars to be launched simultaneously in seven European countries the following Autumn. The project was the result of collaboration between United British Automobiles plc (UBA), the dominant manufacturer in the UK market, and the Sunrise Corporation (SC) of Japan, whose car making division enjoyed a similar position in that country.

The two companies had come together motivated, in the case of UBA, by the need to share the enormous cost of developing and producing a completely new 'family' of cars and, in the case of the SC, by a need to find a way round tariff barriers which were going up in Europe to protect home industries from Japanese competition as the recession deepened. It had therefore been a rather uneasy alliance for the five years during which the cars had been developed and, now that the launch was imminent, tension and friction within the Anglo-Japanese management team was intensifying.

A particular source of conflict was the increasingly acrimonious debate within the two parent companies over the name to be given to the new models, which had hitherto been referred to by the engineering code designation CB84L. It was with the intention of resolving the disagreement and finalizing the programme to be followed in generating and selecting the name that the managing director of UBA had asked his marketing director, Mark Green, to draft a memo he could send to the president of the automobile division of the SC which set out clearly and in detail the path to be followed.

No one knew better than the Managing Director that time was now becoming very pressing indeed. With little more than eight months before the launch it was not possible to finalize advertising, promotion, sales and PR campaigns for either trade or consumer consumption because the models remained unnamed. He was glad, therefore, when Green raised the matter again at a routine Monday morning progress meeting and explained that unless this apparently straightforward matter was resolved soon the entire launch could be in jeopardy.

In discussion Green pointed out that the Japanese company had always found it simple to name their products for English speaking and European markets. Without conducting elaborate, time consuming and expensive research they had chosen model names like 'Cherry', 'Laurel' and 'Sunny' for the UK and other European markets, sometimes with national variants, which were rewarded with commercial sales success. This contrasted with the practice of European manufacturers taking immense care to find names with the right 'image'. For the SC the idea that a product or brand name might have a profound positive or negative influence on sales was almost unheard of and they were therefore unsympathetic to UK concern on this point. While conceding that this attitude stemmed partly from cultural differences, Mike Green suspected that SC executives were blinding themselves to the fact that other aspects of the Japanese 'consumer proposition', such as the price and reliability of the cars, had been sufficiently strong to overcome negative customer feelings about names which sounded fey, effete or feminine in markets where thrusting, aggressive and masculine model names are common.

He argued that because the new range would not be obviously 'Japanese', which all agreed was on balance a marketing plus point, it would be unwise to assume that the cars could ride on the back of this established Japanese reputation. With American experience of a number of model name disasters firmly in mind, Green had dug in his heels in negotiations with the SC to date. He had insisted that a thorough programme of name creation, screening and research was carried out before a proposed name was submitted for the approval of the boards of the partner companies. He believed this was particularly critical because of the intention, which had large potential marketing communications benefits, to use a single model name throughout Europe. His Japanese colleagues regarded this insistence as financially wasteful, unnecessarily time consuming and bureaucratic.

John Clark, the Managing Director, believed that Green had been right to take the stand he had and said that he would back this line in his memo to the president of the SC. In giving additional guidance to Green in drafting the memo, which in view of the relationship between the partners would need to be very tactfully phrased, Clark stressed that any communications research programme would rely heavily on specialist advice on marketing research techniques and trade mark registration. The memo, he said, should cover the following aspects:

1 Why the UK company considered it essential to carry out a comprehensive research and screening process before selecting a model name.

2 How the list of names to be researched would be drawn up.
3 The techniques to be used and the cost and time scale of the operation.
4 The particular difficulties likely to be associated with selecting a single name for use in seven countries.

Question

Draft the memo John Clark has asked for.

Approach

The approach in this case is really dictated by the aspects that the Managing Director suggested should be covered in the Clark memo. You should, therefore, read the signposts given to you by the examiner.

The aspects are in logical sequence and you must decide on a suitable writing style. You should not be fooled by the word 'memo' into thinking that a report format is not necessary. In this case a report-like format is justified in order to make appropriate points on each aspect.

A sensible approach would be to take each aspect and draw up a mini-situation analysis. Each heading in the analysis should be weighted in your own mind as to its importance as supported by evidence derived from the case.

You might then arrange these in a priority order, maybe deleting some which appear to be irrelevant after the first reading, and then start into the question.

The sections should be quite brief and as the recipient is a very senior executive you must remember what you are trying to do. It may be to: .

Inform
Explain
Persuade.

So think carefully:

What does the president know?
What are his attitudes?
What does he really want?

Note that you are given the information that Green's Japanese colleagues regard his insistence as financially wasteful, unnecessarily time consuming and bureaucratic.

These are vital clues. So is the fact that Green suspected that the Japanese were blinding themselves to the fact that other aspects of their 'consumer proposition' overcame negative customer feelings concerning the name. The President must be a busy man.

The order of importance of the aspects would most likely be:

Aspect 1 ⎫ equal importance
Aspect 2 ⎦ equal importance
Aspect 3   most important
Aspect 4   least important

but they must be dealt with in the order that is shown in the case.

Answer

The memo must be easy to read and its structure and content are very important. If you ignore these facts then you will lose easily earned marks.

So, having decided that this memo will cover all the aforementioned communication objectives, a most likely format would be:

To: The President
From: M. Green
Copy: Mr John Clark

Subject: *New European Model Name – Model Code No. CB84L*

This memo is drafted in four sections for your convenience. It is intended to highlight the particular importance that we believe is attached to model names in Europe, give guidelines to how such names can be established, indicate typical costs and time scales, and finally indicate possible difficulties to the intention of using a single model name across Europe.

Section 1   Reasons for name research
Section 2   Naming procedure
Section 3   Testing
Section 4   Evaluation of likely drawbacks

Section 1: underlying reasons for name research

(*a*) The project is nearing completion and it is very necessary to agree our promotional strategy concerning this model.
Vital to this strategy is the model name for the obvious reasons of sales and promotional planning.

(*b*) We operate in a market where aggressive masculine model names are acceptable and dynamic thrusting names commonplace. The reasons are mainly psychological and many theories have been expressed about why this is so. Generally they revolve around personality extension and psychographic profile.

(c) The European culture is such however that lifestyle and class must be recognized together and this is accomplished by a range of possessions – a car being one. Each country has its own perception and expectation of a vehicle which must fit with the culture.

(d) The vehicle will not be recognizable as of Japanese manufacture. Therefore the reliability and price advantage that the European buyer undoubtedly has learned to recognize in such models will not be apparent to him.

(e) *The advantages of reliability and price are being massively eroded as similar cars with equal standards are being produced by other manufacturers.*

For these reasons it is wise to research the acceptability of model name or names before launching the new model. It is also desirable to test our 'brand' image with respect to dilution or reinforcement when using our company name.

Section 2: naming procedure

(a) While marketing executives in both our companies are highly regarded, these proposals should be discussed at the earliest opportunity with specialists in their chosen fields.

(b) Engineers, test track drivers, designers associated with the project in our company will be asked to provide names that they think will serve as model names. Simple suggestion forms are all that are needed. Our employees represent a good cross-section, most of whom are car owners, some even own competitors' models.

Agency personnel and those external agencies who have seen the prototype should be canvassed for possible names. Group discussions, 'brainstorming', synectics, can be used. While we need a certain amount of creativity there will be obvious non-runners which can be filtered out by the marketing department/agency.

We do not expect a 100 per cent response.

(c) There is little point in proceeding unless some form of screening is carried out. At this point our legal department will check ownership of trade marks, names, etc.

(d) The resulting names will be scrutinized by our top dealers, all of whom are aware of the prototype and who value secrecy from the commercial viewpoint. The ten most popular names will be chosen.

(e) Video material already available with our agency will be shown to our target market/segments. These were established when product range and options were jointly agreed.

Sampling and testing procedures will be left to the agency concerned. We will be mindful of two things in briefing them:

- to avoid collusion between dealers;
- to produce clear evidence of name preference;

(i.e., eliminating bias as much as possible either by the research method and/or other content of the pictorial material).

Sample frames are readily available and this work (matching names to pictures, etc. of cars) is speedily carried out.

(f) The same type of research will be carried out in our top two European markets. The favourite name will then be the subject of comment by motoring correspondents in other countries.

Section 3: testing

(a) We are open to any suggestions that our chosen research agency make. However, the law of diminishing returns applies.

If there is no clear-cut evidence coming from simple, clear, easy to apply techniques, then more sophisticated testing may be agreed.

Our own product testing suggests that in performance and specification terms and in quality of engineering, our product is positioned correctly.

If these do not match the perception of the model by name after consumer use, there is no name, however well researched, that will save the product line.

(b) Time-scale is very simple – we have eight months available. Production can transfer or fix name plates on order of the car by dealer *if absolutely necessary. We are too late even now to model name the first production models in factory.*

Marketing department have given a lead time of five months for all promotional material.

The estimate for the research as outlined is ten weeks.

(e) Costs £190,000 ±10% c.f. appendix for more detailed breakdown.

Section 4: evaluation of likely drawbacks

(a) We have given priority to our largest markets, markets where it is likely to assume that our model name will be acceptable. These may not be our fastest growing markets.

(b) In the event that in our secondary markets the name is clearly a mistake our promotional spend can be curtailed until remedial action is taken, i.e. change to model number.

(c) The use of a single model name across Europe may cause us headaches due to misinterpretation, but in terms of impact and awareness is a vital prerequisite to building market share.

(d) The short time scale left to us due to lack of agreement will undoubtedly make the selection of a single name universally accepted across Europe difficult. A postponement of the European launch may be inevitable if the research is inconclusive.

Appendix

Traditionally our advertising research budget has been about 5 per cent of our national media spend. I expect name research to be of the same order. There have been enormous sums of money spent, certainly in corporate name testing, but there is a limit to even my belief in research.

The geographical breakdown is in strict order of expected sales turnover and is related to unit sales in our top markets.

Notes on approach/answer

Here we see a slightly different 'house style' in answering. You can see, however, that the elements of the approach – the use of clear section headings, action, analysis and a professional style – are still all in evidence.

We shall now look at a further sample mini case, and yet another variation on the basic approach.

PLANNING AND CONTROL

Approximate time: 1½ hours

Skinclad Ltd

Section I

Skinclad Ltd has been making high quality leather, suede and sheepskin men's outerwear for over twenty-five years, in old rented premises in the heart of the UK textile industry. The company has a flexible labour force of about fifty employees and three directors, only one of whom, namely Mr Frank, the managing director, is fully active.

The current range consists of jackets and full length coats in twenty-two styles and the company capacity is 400–500 garments per week, depending on style and continuity of the production run. Additional floor space, machinists and machines could be brought into use to raise production to a maximum of 1000 garments weekly.

Trade sources estimated a UK market valued at about £1.5m in 1985 but since then inflation and recession have deflated the market, resulting in many smaller businesses having to cease trading. Census of production figures indicated some 1200 men's outerwear manufacturers, six of which accounted for 25 per cent of output. There were about 1000 small manufacturers employing less than 100, accounting for about 20 per cent of total industry output in the mid-1980s.

Independent menswear shops make 23 per cent of jacket and 30 per cent of coat sales; multiple tailors 15 per cent and 22 per cent; and variety chainstores 12 per cent and 13 per cent respectively. Skinclad's sales were traditionally effected through agents, who tended to change frequently throughout the years. However, in the period 1980 to 1985 Skinclad's production was increasingly taken up by Modal Fashions, a successful clothing chainstore with outlets throughout Europe, and in the 1984–85 financial year they accounted for 93 per cent of gross sales, by which time Skinclad had terminated all but one of their agency agreements.

In 1986, owing to market depression, Modal Fashions drastically reduced their contract quantity to 25 per cent of the previous year and

Skinclad were forced into two-days-a-week production. Although quantities have gradually increased since late 1986, negotiations with Modal Fashions have become more and more difficult, such that the agreed price gives Skinclad a net profit per garment as low as 10p on some styles. Mr Frank suspects that Modal Fashions use Skinclad only as a back-up supplier to much cheaper garments from Korea and Taiwan. It is currently rumoured in the trade that a number of customers are returning Far Eastern made leather garments with complaints of poor stitching and dye running.

An abortive attempt was made in 1986 by Skinclad to export through an overseas factor selling garments to the Norwegian and Swedish markets.

Although Modal Fashions ordered Skinclad garments for sale through their outlets in Belgium, Germany and France in 1984 and orders increased to an embarrassing level, the flow suddenly dried up without explanation although no complaints had been received.

Since 1985 Skinclad had traded around breakeven levels and are working within a bank overdraft of £50,000 and reduced credit levels from suppliers.

Skinclad's bankers have recently asked for a meeting with Mr Frank to discuss both the overdraft and the future prospects of the company. The lease on Skinclad's premises is due for renewal at the end of this year. Mr Frank has, in some desperation, called in the services of a marketing consultancy for advice.

In the role of the marketing consultant, draft an initial report to Mr Frank which:

(a) Reviews the environmental factors which are likely to impact upon Skinclad's business over the next five years. (*15 marks*)
(b) Suggests objectives in light of the above review and the current company situation which you feel are achievable over the next five years. (*10 marks*)
(c) Indicates possible courses of action to profitably increase sales in the short term within Skinclad's current production and financial constraints and suggests how Mr Frank might proceed to evaluate these opportunities. (*25 marks*)

Notes on approach

Here are the key pointers in the case and questions which you need to take into account.

In the role of the marketing consultant you must draft an initial report to Mr Frank which:

(a) Reviews the environmental factors which are likely to impact upon Skinclad's business over the next five years. (*15 marks*)

Approach

A straightforward question calling for the listing of the environmental factors which affect all businesses but with the detail taking into account the size and nature of the company featured in the case.

(*b*) Suggests objectives in light of the above review and the current company situation which you feel are achievable over the next five years. (*10 marks*)

Approach

Operative words are 'in light of' calling for harmonization of objectives with review plus realistic tailoring to the current and likely future situation in the medium term. Clearly objectives need to be set on the theme of profitably increasing sales in view of the statement made in (*c*).

(*c*) Indicates possible courses of action to profitably increase sales in the short term within Skinclad's current production and financial constraints and suggests how Mr Frank might proceed to evaluate these opportunities. (*25 marks*)

Approach

This is a two-part question calling for proposals on the one hand and how to evaluate these proposals on the other hand. Actions need to be constrained by current production and financial limitations. At this draft stage a wide range of suggested actions is appropriate.

Answer

Draft initial report

From: Marketing Consultant
To: Managing Director, Skinclad Ltd
Date: 17th June, 1987

Contents

Foreword
Part A   Review of environmental factors

Part B   Objectives 1987–1992
Part C   Proposed actions and methods of evaluation

Foreword

This being an initial report, the contents are relatively brief and intended to serve as discussion points to facilitate the identification of key areas for subsequent detailed examination.

The initial review of environmental factors is seen as necessary for medium-term objectives and strategies but most of these will not seriously affect the existing business in the short term.

Clearly 'survival bids' are short-term actions and we need to concentrate on turning round the existing situation or breakeven trading to one of profitable trading as soon as possible with a view to placating the bank and justifying the renewal of the lease. For this reason a wide variety of alternative short-term actions has been listed which we need to discuss in order to ascertain viabilities, ease/difficulty of putting into motion and to evaluate likely cost/profit ratios. Following this discussion we could set priorities and proceed on a trial basis over the next six months. If we plan this well – and I am very willing to assist further in this respect – then it is likely that the bank will view kindly the renewal of the overdraft at a slightly higher level in order to finance these initiatives, in their longer term interests.

Part A: review of environmental factors

A1 *Social factors*: Possible fashion changes, consumerism (anti-animal skin lobby), population trends, attitudes towards quality, etc.
A2 *Legal factors*: Animal protection laws, motorcycle regulations, company trading laws, international trade regulations, etc.
A3 *Political trends*: Government protection of home markets, aid to small companies, changes in government at national and local level. Complete harmonization of EEC trade.
A4 *Economic factors*: State of UK economy, taxes, interest rates, GNP, discretionary incomes, etc. State of potential export markets, currency changes, etc.
A5 *Technological factors*: New production machinery, robotics, computers, synthetic leathers/suedes, competitors home and abroad, changes in retailing, etc.

Part B: objectives 1987–1992

B1   *Short-term objectives 1987–88*
B1.1 To profitably increase sales from the current level of £N to £N plus 10 per cent by the end of this financial year and £N plus 25 per cent by the end of 1988, mainly through quality retail outlets.
B2   *Medium term objectives 1988–1992*
B2.1 To increase profitability from the current breakeven level to above the level of building society interest rates by 1992.
B2.2 To reduce dependence on current products by diversifying into other products such as women's outerwear or fabric rather than animal skin outerwear starting immediately.
B2.3 To reduce dependence on Modal Fashions to a maximum of 50 per cent of turnover by 1992.

Part C: proposed actions/evaluation methods

C1   To export to European multiple outlets – evaluate through BOTB and personal visits to establish cost/price levels.
C2   To exhibit at fashion shows – check with specialist magazines for show details, organizers for costs and other exhibitors for sales potential and evaluate profit possibilities.
C3   Arrange own fashion presentations to selected multiples – evaluate on trial basis.
C4   Open up the factory as a shop selling direct to local public at weekends – place advertisements in local paper and open up on a trial basis.
C5   Make women's outerwear using existing skills and materials and the advice of a fashion consultant. Evaluate by personal survey of major UK retail outlets.
C6   Try smaller up-market mail order companies for contracts for men's and women's outerwear – evaluate by making appointments and personally visiting buyers with samples.
C7   Advertise a particular garment in a limited range of colours in the Sunday newspapers as a direct mail order venture – evaluate by discussion with newspaper experts responsible.
C8   Seek to re-establish agency network – advertise in specialist magazine or identify most successful agents and head-hunt through recruitment experts. Evaluate by discussion with selected prospective agents the sales prospects, prices and profitability potential.
C9   Having designed women's leather/suede outerwear and organized fashion shows to selected multiples, try fashion shows on smaller scale

either at factory at weekends or during week at Women's Institutes and other social centres.

C10 Employ salesforce of people with contacts on a high commission basis – evaluate as C8.

C11 Seek franchises or concessions in the form of shops within shops – host shops to supply staff, we to supply stock on sale or return basis. Evaluate by discussion with selected department stores.

C12 Introduce range of specialized motorcycle garments marketed through motorcycle outlets/clubs – seek specialist agent and evaluate as C8.

C13 Introduce range of mixed leather/suede and other fabric garments aimed at fashion conscious upmarket young males and females. Seek advice of specialist designers and evaluate as for C5.

C14 Introduce leather/suede accessories, e.g. belts, handbags, hats, wallets, etc. on trial basis and sell as coordinated ensembles.

C15 Investigate possibilities of commercial links with other non-leather/suede quality garment manufacturers with established retail outlets in the USA. Identify through BOTB and personally visit to evaluate potential.

C16 Produce detailed marketing research and credible marketing plans in order to secure higher overdraft facilities and negotiate better credit deals with suppliers.

6

SELECTED MINI CASES WITH SPECIMEN ANSWERS

By now you should have a good grasp of the nature of mini cases and how to tackle them. In approaching mini cases, in earlier chapters you were given an insight into how a candidate might approach them through comprehensive notes and pointers.

In this chapter we have selected three of the Institute's diploma mini cases, again one for each subject, and included a specimen answer without accompanying notes and guidance.

These are intended to give you a clear indication of what a good examination answer would look like, without the added complications of notes/comments, etc. Again, you should note that the specimen answers which accompany the cases are for your guidance and should not be considered as perfect solutions.

As mentioned earlier, to get the most out of this text it is a good idea to work through each of the cases in turn on your own, preparing your own analysis and answers, and then comparing your response with the specimen solution.

In order to help you with this preparation, and indeed for the examination itself, the Appendix to this text includes details of how to set out a report. You can turn to this as required.

Remember, too, that you have one and a half hours in which to complete your mini-case examination and this includes reading and comprehension time, so do not spend an undue amount of time on each of the cases. Do not be put off by the fact that it is unlikely that you will be able to complete as much as is written in the 'model' solution. The solutions were not written under examination conditions and are supposed to represent the 'ideal' comprehensive answer. What you should look for when you read this solution is *structure*, and whether or not your answer has followed a similar structure. It is highly unlikely that you will have been able to write as much as the solutions.

This case has, of course, been used earlier by way of illustration in terms of the examiner's report, so you should be familiar with where students went wrong.

MARKETING MANAGEMENT – PLANNING AND CONTROL
Approximate time: 1½ hours

Olworth Leisure Centre

There are several hundred leisure/sports/recreation centres in the UK jointly provided by public authorities and local education authorities.

A typical centre includes a sports hall, swimming pool, two gymnasia, squash courts, sauna, solarium, lounge bar and games area and is located in a surrounding fielded area for track sports and athletics. The indoor sports hall would be marked out for badminton, netball, volleyball, etc. and might be large enough for an occasional indoor tennis court.

Olworth is a population centre of about 10,000 inhabitants and considered to be an area of high deprivation and isolation, resulting in relatively high rates of crime and vandalism. Most of the menfolk work in nearby coalmines on a shift system.

The district council responsible for Olworth are considering building a leisure centre in the conurbation for use by its local population, but with the hope of attracting people from surrounding villages and hamlets within a radius of ten miles with an additional population of 12,000. Owing to financial and other constraints building is likely to take place in three phases over a total of three years.

Obviously objectives for the provision and use of leisure centre services are not necessarily based upon profit as such, although a level of income contributing considerably towards running costs is projected.

Leisure centre services are not always in a situation of economic balance where demand matches supply and it is not unusual for some activities/ facilities to be overbooked (e.g., squash and swimming) while other minority sports facilities are grossly under-utilised. A major problem facing local authority-provided centres has been the maximization of usage during weekdays. In the evenings and weekend, with the demand from the general public and various clubs and organizations, the space more than sells itself.

Olworth Council see this project somewhat as a marketing planning and control exercise. They are anxious to achieve a good match between supply and demand and are aware of the importance of the four Ps (place being in the sense of timing of a given leisure facility and its duration as well as location) in this aim. They have asked a local college to put this project to their Diploma in Marketing course members in the hope of obtaining some practical help in the form of a marketing plan. As a member of this course your individual task is to:

(a) Suggest suitable corporate objectives for the proposed leisure centre. (*10 marks*)
(b) Write a brief for a marketing research plan with the aim of identifying target markets for various leisure/sports/recreational facilities. (*15 marks*)
(c) Outline a promotional plan to communicate with these target audiences with a budgeted spend of only £10,000 covering the three months pre-opening and three months post-opening period. (*25 marks*)

Answer

To: Olworth Council
From: Diploma in Marketing Course Members
Date: 11th June, 1986

Proposed marketing plan: Olworth Leisure Centre

Part A: corporate objectives

A1 To maximize the use of the centre's facilities.
A2 To cater for the widest possible leisure requirements of the community at large.
A3 To provide for minority activities as well as popular ones.
A4 To obtain an income for the use of the facilities high enough to offset most of the running costs without effectively freezing out deprived families.
A5 To help to reduce crime and vandalism by providing alternative occupations of leisure time.
A6 To increase community awareness and usage of leisure facilities provided by Olworth Council.
A7 Other.

Part B: brief for marketing research plan

Aim To identify target markets for various leisure/sports/recreational facilities consistent with the above objectives.

B1 *Internal/desk research*
Collect information on:
B1.1 Similar leisure centre provisions and take-ups.
B1.2 Demographic characteristics of people/households within defined catchment areas.
B1.3 Consumer/customer profiles for different types of leisure/sports/ recreational activities for matching against B1.2.
B1.4 Infrastructure of catchment area including industrial/commercial concerns, transport facilities, roads, etc.
B1.5 Competitive leisure/sports/recreational facilities within catchment area.
B1.6 Proposed facilities for Olworth Leisure Centre – those considered mandatory and those considered optional.
B1.7 Constraints on use of facilities – maximum usage possible.
B1.8 Existing promotional facilities available in addition to budgeted spend.
B.2 *External/field research*
B2.1 Visits by council staff to similar leisure centres. (See B.1.1.)
B2.2 Brief marketing research agencies for costs involved in conducting a survey on a representative sample of the target markets within the catchment area to elicit:
   B2.2.1 Numbers and types of people wanting to use each proposed facility.
   B2.2.2 Times of day, days of week they want to use each facility.
   B2.2.3 Price levels expected for each facility and conditioning usage.
   B2.2.4 What services and other expectations do people have of a successful leisure centre?
   B2.2.5 Media read, watched, heard by these intending users.
B2.3 Timing considerations.
B2.4 Report format considerations. Number of reports needed and to whom to be presented.
B2.5 Select agency.

Part C: outline promotional plan (budget £10,000)

C1 Promotional objectives.
C2 Identified target audiences (ex-marketing research plan).
C3 Local media reading/watching/listening habits by market segment (e.g., children aged X to Y).
C4 Creative platform.
C5 Promotional spend by element of mix: pre- and post-opening:

		Pre- opening £	Post- opening £
C5.1	Personal selling (visits, talks, etc.)	X	X
C5.2	PR – press releases and receptions	X	X
C5.3	Leaflets	X	X
C5.4	Posters	X	X
C5.5	Direct mail shots	X	X
C5.6	Local cinema	X	X
C5.7	Exhibitions, videos	X	X
C5.8	Public address vehicles hire and usage	X	X
C5.9	Press/magazine advertising	X	X
C5.10	Special offers, competitors	X	X
C5.11	Opening celebrations	X	—
C6	Timing considerations.		
C7	Contingency reserves/plan.		
C8	Promotional efficiency measures/tracking research.		
C9	Agency briefs.		
C10	Agency selection.		

MARKETING COMMUNICATIONS

Approximate time: 1½ hours

Wings

Behind the scenes at Wings a 'family' of 2000 professional airline people spend their working lives making sure that business and holiday travellers have smooth flights from the moment of check-in to disembarking. Wings' headquarters is located close to London's Gatwick Airport. The fleet of Boeing 737s, Lockheed Tristars and Boeing 747 Jumbos are fine tuned, fussed over and pampered like children. Wings is a far bigger airline than most people imagine. It is the fourth largest carrier in the UK holiday market, carrying over 1,000,000 passengers annually. As a wholly owned subsidiary of a major British airline Wings have immense expertise in engineering, flight operations and safety.

Wings have a sophisticated image, which distinguishes them from many charter airlines, brought about partly from their continued financial success.

A little known fact is that Wings operate a whole network of scheduled services to eighteen European destinations, apart from international charter flights.

Wings conduct engineering and servicing work for other airlines at their modern engineering base at Gatwick, but Wings is best known among travel agents as a holiday airline, the one associated with lazy days on sun-saturated beaches in far-flung destinations.

As Wings' Managing Director, 39-year-old Terry Forbes explains, 'One of our future goals is further development of the long-haul market. We have the backing – now we need the takers. In addition to our established US flights to Los Angeles, San Francisco, Tampa and Miami, East Africa and the Indian Ocean are key targets. Nationally, oveer 250,000 Britons took long-haul holidays this year – a growth of 20 per cent on last year'.

Wings are conscious of their public image – considerable attention is devoted to their corporate livery. A high percentage of their existing customers are first-time fliers or those who fly just once a year – mostly package holiday takers.

Wings, as a passenger carrier only, provides charter aircraft for a wide range of British tour operators. They do not provide complete holiday packages, because 'Flying' is their business. Among their 200 pilots the minimum length of flying experience is fifteen years; of the 240 skilled engineers some boast over thirty years service. 'Our staff training features the needs of the leisure traveller. With up to 3500 people passing through Gatwick in a peak hour and Wings handling business for over twenty other airlines at our many check-ins we come into contact with over six million passengers a year. We put people first!'

Question

Terry Forbes is anxious to build an increased awareness for Wings as an airline and also for the range of services the company offers:

(*a*) To the travel trade.
(*b*) To the business and leisure traveller.

Advise him of your recommendations in a structured marketing communications plan.

Answer

To: T. Forbes
From: Diploma in Marketing Course Members
Date: 11th June, 1987

Marketing communications plan: Wings

Part A: general observations

A1 Wings needs to develop a heightened awareness for the airline per se and for sales of the range of services available to the travel trade and the travellers.
A2 Substantial resources underpin the company. These arise from the history of the organisation and the financial growth record to date.
A3 Wings have a sound credibility base from which to build marketing and marketing communications initiatives (albeit in a price sensitive market).
A4 Currently Wings as an airline is a carrier and should *not* be confused

with tour operators who conduct business in the total package holiday market.

Part B: marketing communications plan

B1   *Marketing research*
Before proceeding with the design/development of the communications plan it is recommended that the following research be conducted to provide a database.

B1.1 *Researching the travel trade*
The following information is required to provide a benchmark for subsequent research initiatives.
B1.1.1 Prevailing attitudes towards Wings.
B1.1.2 How Wings is perceived compared to other carriers.
B1.1.3 Knowledge of Wings' services.
B1.1.4 Reasons for use, continued use or lapsed use of Wings' services.
B1.1.5 Key buying motives.

B1.2 *Researching the consumer*
The consumer group comprises:
B1.2.1 The leisure traveller/associated DMU
B1.2.2 The business traveller/associated DMU
A distinction must be drawn between the buyer of scheduled services and the buyer of package holidays. In the case of the latter the buyer buys a total branded package often from the high street travel agent and would not select an airline on which to travel. This is not the case with the booking of scheduled flights.

The research should therefore be conducted among both groups to determine:

1 Knowledge of airlines (brands).
2 Perception of those airlines.
3 Preference for travel on selected airlines.
4 Purchase motivations of those specified airlines.
5 Knowledge of and attitudes towards Wings.

The findings of both pieces of research will indicate the nature of the marketing communications task to be undertaken and from this a budget level can be proposed to achieve the communications tasks specified. It is recommended that a high profile market research agency be appointed to match the corporate profile of Wings and that an eight-week period be devoted to this research from briefing to receiving the market report.

B2　*Assumptions*
B2.1 The research programme as proposed is adopted.
B2.2 The budgetary level for marketing communications is accepted and available for deployment.
B2.3 The time scale for the plan is twelve months.
B2.4 Full corporate commitment is received for these initiatives.
B2.5 This is the first time that the company has addressed this problem.
B2.6 The corporate objectives specified by Terry Forbes, Wings' MD, are firm intentions and not wishful thinking.
B3　*Corporate objectives*
B3.1 To reposition Wings as a known, established, national/international carrier to the travel trade.
B3.2 To penetrate the long-haul holiday market.
B3.3 Through 3.1 and 3.2 to sustain the financial achievement of the airline as a total business entry.
B4　*Marketing objectives*
　　　Arising from the corporate objectives:
B4.1 Improve market share in the tour operator market segment.
B4.2 Penetrate further the long-haul destination market.
B4.3 Increase awareness of and improve attitude towards Wings as a safe, efficient airline.
B5　*Budgetary considerations*
　　　In view of the scale of the perceived communications tasks and the size of Wings' airline plus the support of Wings' parent company, it is envisaged that the size of the advertising budget will be substantial, and sufficient to achieve the tasks specified. It is assumed therefore that the plan will not be constrained by a modest budget.
B6　*Marketing communications objectives*
　　　Based upon the prescribed research and results obtained:
B6.1 Project a revised image of Wings to the travel trade.
B6.2 Achieve a marked change in knowledge of Wings/Wings' services among the travel trade.
B6.3 Achieve and maintain a favourable disposition for Wings among tour operators as a safe, effective airline.
B6.4 Improve knowledge of and attitudes towards Wings by:
　　　B6.4.1 The leisure traveller
　　　B6.4.2 The business traveller
　　　within a twelve-month time scale and budgetary levels.
B7　*Target market specifications*
B7.1 Target market group – the travel trade:
　　　B7.1.1 Tour operators who both use, have used or may use Wings as a package holiday carrier/or those involved in long-haul packages. (Key target – persons/DMU involved in tour decisions and promotion decisions.)

Justification for selection: Wings are *not* in the holiday package business but provide 'transport' to specific destinations. This is a new business direction and they need to penetrate the decision making process, including facilitators in the decision process at the point of sales.

B7.1.2 Travel agents who support and promote those tour operators' holiday packages with whom Wings is now working. (Key target – travel agents, managers/counter staff.)

Justification for selection: This segment *must* receive specific attention. It is a core market.

B7.2 Target market group – the leisure traveller:

B7.2.1 The leisure traveller who purchases a package.

Justification for selection: To ensure that leisure travellers are confident in travelling with Wings.

B7.2.2 The leisure traveller who purchases a scheduled airline ticket.

Justification for selection: To penetrate this segment, discriminate favourably towards Wings as an airline.

B7.3 Target market group – the business traveller who buys scheduled air flights.

Justification for selection: To penetrate this segment which has freedom of choice we need such buyers to discriminate favourably towards Wings as an airline.

B8 *Agency dynamics*

It is proposed that this campaign be handled by an international full service agency with experience in marketing international airlines.

B8.1 Wings is an international operator and needs international coverage for the campaign at points of destination as well as points of departure.

B8.2 The profile of the company warrants a large, high profile agency.

B8.3 Additional services in the extended market of communications mix may (will) be needed and it is more cost effective to work through one agency.

B9 *Creative interpretations*

B9.1 The research programme will input ideas on buyer motivations to fuel the creative interpretation of the campaign.

B9.2 Wings are in the 'geographic transfer of people business'. The business must be seen therefore as highly personalized, caring, safe, secure, honest, trustworthy, efficient and presentable.

B9.3 Images of these qualitative components must be interpreted and conveyed in the creative planning and execution of the campaign.

B9.4 The interpretation must be visually consistent with the themes to be delivered.

B9.5 To carry the main advertising theme, a distinctive slogan for both trade/consumer is needed. Corporate livery is already well established; therefore no change at this stage is recommended. However close association with corporate livery and the main slogan *is* essential.

B9.6 The major problem arising is that many "people-related themes" have already been used by competitors. For example:

- We take more care of you.
- We treat you like gold.
- You arrive in better shape with . . . .

B9.7 Therefore Wings must position the airline to gain distinction. For example:

- 'Wings – carries you in comfort, in time – an experience you remember to depend upon!'

B10 *Above-the line*

B10.1 *Media selection*: national TV:
30-second commercials scheduled to peak buying times during the trading year.
Justification: Corporate level advertising is essential to increase awareness among all target groups and to lay the foundation for subsequent supporting advertising to distinct segments.

B10.2 Media selection – press:
B10.2.1 *National*
Justification: To support the TV campaign. The popular daily press will reach the leisure travellers and travel trade.
B10.2.2 *Business*
Justification: Targeted to reach the discerning buyers of scheduled air flights.
B10.2.3 *Trade press/directories*
Justification: to reach tour operators and the travel trade.

B10.3 *Media selection*: National poster campaign
Justification: To support the TV campaign and increase awareness of Wings as an international carrier of stature.

B10.4 Outline media schedule:

	Jul.	Aug.	Sep.	Oct.	Nov.	Dec.	Jan.	Feb.	Mar.	Apr.	May
TV					———————						
Press consumer			———————								
Business			————			————————					
Trade	——										
Posters					———————						

Notes: The advertising is scheduled to peak in January 1988, a time of peak buying in the package tour business and leisure traveller business. The business press is designed for two bursts to cover six months of the year.

Trade press/trade directory advertising will be carried through the year. The poster campaign will support the peak time exposure and be extended to assist the carry-over effect of TV advertising.

B11   *Below-the-line activity*

It is assumed that the company has established point-of-sale display material which carries the company corporate livery. This may now need to be changed to project and convey a more modern image. It is not envisaged at this time to *concentrate* on a programme of heavy sales promotion to the consumer because the communications task at this time is one of *corporate* communications. It would be wrong to confuse this with a programme of consumer/dealer incentives.

B12   *Public relations*

The marketing communications objectives previously specified have been embodied in the above/below-the-line activity outlined above. The PR objectives support these marketing communications objectives and achieve a climate of informed opinion between Wings and the many publics with whom and to whom the organization relates in the context of this campaign. It is not envisaged at this stage to change with existing internal PR activities. The essential task is viewed therefore as one of external corporate PR.

PR activities	*Publics*		
	The trade	*Leisure*	*Business*
B12.1 *Personal*:			
The level of personal contact with the trade needs to be improved to achieve wider communications objectives	X		
Facility visits, conventions and free visits to new locations are to be encouraged to maximize high level contact between Wings' executives and key members of the travel trade, including tour operators and travel agents.	X		
B12.2 *Printed*:	*The trade*	*Leisure*	*Business*
Full use of printed forms of PR must be used to get newsworthy items across to all prescribed publics.	X	X	X
The revised corporate image must be explained and conveyed effectively and honestly.	X	X	X

B12.2	The trade	Leisure	Business
Above all a new stance must be *seen* to be taken, implemented *and* maintained. Use of news releases and editorials for selected press must be used to maximize publicity in selected press. A presence must be felt in printed form *throughout* the 12-month period, *not* just on a casual basis.			

B12.3 *Visual*:

	The trade	Leisure	Business
The existing corporate livery is the vehicle to carry through the heightened profits of Wings.	X	X	X

The new slogan, following board approval and following consumer/ trade concept tests, should be adopted and be seen on all company communications instruments so that all publicity is in contact with the revised corporate message.

B13   *Selling*

The modification to company communications must be manifest in the selling process to all target market segments. The 'in-house magazine' wil be used to explain the changes but all personnel must receive a briefing on the rationale for the change, so that a consistent, united view is presented to all company prospects.

B14   *Effectiveness measures*

The objectives set for the communications plan should be measurable and achievable. These were based upon benchmarks identified through the process of market research prior to the campaign.

    Qualitative motivational research should be used again at the end of the campaign period to assess the changes which have been achieved (if any).

B15   *Budget breakdown*

Communication plan elements	*% Allocation*	*Rationale*
Above-the-line	70	The major task facing Wings is to improve the awareness of the airline and to encourage more long-haul tour business. This therefore *needs* heavy above-the-line advertising; hence the 70% allocation.

B15   *Budget breakdown*

Communication plan elements	*% Allocation*	*Rationale*
Below-the-line	10	Little to be initiated. A higher per cent allocation will be needed in year 2 when selling into the long-haul market.
Public relations	20	20% allocated to support the corporate nature of the airline marketing communications programme.

Budget level

No indication is given in the information provided to the writer. The assumption is that the budget would be substantial. It is thought that an appropriate level to achieve the stated objectives would be £1.5–2m.

INTERNATIONAL ASPECTS OF MARKETING
Approximate time: 1½ hours

Interdecor Designs Ltd

Interdecor Designs is a small but successful firm of interior designers in the United Kingdom, specializing in the creation and implementation of top grade room designs and furnishings for hotels and public rooms. Three women (one an architect, the second an interior designer and the third a furnishing materials specialist) had combined their respective talents to form their company some five years ago and had successfully carried out a number of contracts for hotels around the country. They were able to offer a complete design service: from the original design or redesign of a room and its furnishings; the acquisition of suitable materials and furniture, including original designs where necessary; and the supervision of the actual contract work up to the final completion and handing over to the client. Contract prices were agreed with the client according to the nature and size of the job, together with expenses and commission on purchases. Although sufficient business had developed to keep the three partners active, the current economic climate in the UK, though improving, did not show much prospect for expansion.

This was the topic of discussion during a partners' get-together.

'I think we ought to start looking abroad for some more business. During my summer holiday in Europe, I stayed in a number of hotels which were very pleasant, but there were several which could have been considerably improved without much difficulty or great expense. Those French wallpapers, for instance – huge bouquets of flowers, row upon row of them, all round the room – I lay in bed one night and counted them. Regular patterns are all very well, but this was in a converted seventeenth century chateau. None of the rooms was square, the patterns went everywhere; and as for the pink plastic lampshades, the whole effect was crude and disturbing instead of being restful; it certainly was not in keeping with the rest of the place. We could do so much for them.'

'But perhaps that is French taste – it was graded as a second class local hotel, not truly international ones like the Hiltons or Holiday Inns, for example. Their rooms are almost identical in whichever country they are situated. What scope is there for us in a completely standardized approach?'

'But their public rooms try to reflect local tastes or features – the group hotels often have their own centralized design departments to do so. Now, if we could get in with one of them, in Europe or elsewhere . . . .'

'But I prefer dealing with individually owned places – these give me far more scope and flexibility.'

'You would really need to know local tastes and cultures then; they are often very traditional, more like domestic designing.'

'We have already found that domestic designs can be very interesting and profitable. Look at that stately home we did last year; it was almost a palace by the time we had finished.'

'Talking of palaces, I wonder if there are any being built just now in the Middle East? I have always been fascinated by Islamic architecture and think of the prestige for British designers if we could do one – even a few rooms.'

'Prestige is all very well, but the firm I used to work for had a contract out there before I joined them; everything was sent out but there was a long delay for some reason; by the time the crates were opened all the foam back carpeting had deteriorated in the heat; the glues and finishes had dried out and to add insult to injury, the termites had made a meal of some Chippendale chairs.'

'Give me Germany any time: even if the building regulations are different in each area, at least it is closer to the UK, especially for supervision.'

'What about the costs involved? You know that we have only budgeted for £1000 for you to travel abroad, plus any grants that we can obtain.'

'That money was for travelling and prospecting for customers; the supervision would be included in the contract, but you have a point there. Perhaps we ought to look at leisure centres in major holiday resort countries? The field could be wide open for us, with all that building going on in Spain for instance.'

They all agreed that, while continuing with their work within the UK, it seemed that there could be some very good opportunities for their design services abroad in a number of countries. What they now needed was advice on possible clients and a plan to market their services to the best advantages.

Questions

The questions below draw attention to some international aspects of the situation, *all* of which you are required to answer. There are other aspects relevant to the possible development of the firm's activities which you may wish to consider and credit will be given for suitable observations.

Advise Interdecor on:

(*a*) A research procedure into cultures, tastes and requirements in particular selected country(ies) (35%)

(*b*) An outline marketing plan for the overseas development of their services. (35%)

(*c*) Publicity and advertising in respect of overseas business. (20%)

Additional observations and presentation. (10%)

Answer

Recommendations to the firm of Interdecor Designs Ltd on their proposals for overseas operations.

1 Introduction

Before considering making any recommendations, the report first considers the present situation of the firm, as there are some significant features apparent which will influence the approach to carrying out the marketing research, the formulation of a company plan and the possible promotional activities. These are detailed below:

1.1 The current management strength: all three partners are specialists in their own right and there is no particular evidence of significant marketing expertise other than their present level of success in the UK.

1.2 There is also evidence of their lack of knowledge of international constraints and market forces.

1.3 The existing business is stated to be 'keeping the partners active'.

1.4 The evidence suggests that any funds for the development of the business are limited (e.g., the £1,000 limit for foreign travel).

1.5 The company is currently marketing a design and contracting service, in which the accent is on the service element arising from the personal flair and expertise of the partners.

1.6 The various limitations of finance, personnel and other resources, taken with the nature of their business, points toward the search for a few contracts only, possibly three or four in any one year; otherwise the individual specialists will be too stretched. Either their work could suffer or alternatively they would need to increase their staff and this may or may not be desirable.

2 Research procedure into culture, tastes and requirements in particular selected country(ies)

Note: It has been assumed from the information available to the writer that the particular target country or more than one has been selected. At this stage, therefore, the following recommendations are made only with respect to a recommended procedure within the chosen country.

2.1 The first stage must be to examine the partners' existing knowledge. Information is given that at least two of the staff have either been abroad or been involved in overseas negotiations. This must have given them at least a minimum working knowledge of the situation in their selected country. This should be evaluated and use made of any personal or business contacts who could add to their knowledge.

2.2 Literature can be obtained on all countries mentioned from public libraries or booksellers. Art and travel books may be obtained which could provide the necessary background knowledge and if, as may often be the case, these may be dated, then national government offices (such as that for France in Piccadilly, London) or indeed private and general travel agencies, have many brochures or booklets which will assist. Such information is usually either free or available at a nominal cost.

2.3 As part of their national publicity and promotional campaign to encourage foreign visitors, the government office should be able to supply information on particular rebuilding or renovation activities in their public sector, as well as national and local schemes for private developments. While there may be some reluctance to consider a foreign firm, the experience of the designers, supported by suitable illustrations of their past work, may show their skills and secure for them at least more serious discussions on possible opportunities.

2.4 The French are very interested in their heritage, both buildings and decor, and of appropriate artefacts and design schemes; and research into the publications of the French equivalents of *Home and Garden* magazines or of their National Trust should give many insights into current trends. Such journals also frequently include publicity articles and advertisements for firms, together with the services offered. These references may be useful leads to possible work for Interdecor.

2.5 An alternative source of information within this country could be British building firms or architectural designers who have been engaged in such activities. The Royal Institute of British Architects and Designers, to which the partners probably belong, should be able to provide details of such firms as well as current advice on problems arising. This service should be available to them as members.

2.6 At this stage, a visit to the BOTB could be appropriate. The firm will by now have obtained a good background knowledge but may need detailed information on particular aspects. Initially, they should contact their nearest regional office for advice. This could lead to referral to the Export for Europe.

Assuming that the above mentioned activities result in a number of possible contacts, these could be reduced in number by correspondence. The shortlist of possibilities could then be approached in person by one of the partners for more detailed discussions. It is most likely that the BOTB could supply financial assistance to carry out the research. Any technical or local design problems could probably be resolved through the Technical Help branch.

3 Outline marketing plan for the owners' development of company services

Note: Apart from continuing with their activities with the United Kingdom, the proposal to go abroad will require careful preparation and planning. The following is an outline of recommendations for your marketing plan.

3.1 *Situation analysis*

3.1.1 The current business prospects for Interdecor in the United Kingdom indicate that whilst the firm is likely to be able to continue in business there are no great prospects for any appreciable development and expansion.

3.1.2 Preliminary investigations indicate that there could be possible opportunities in France, Germany and Spain. Countries further afield are not to be considered at this stage because of logistical problems.

3.1.3 There are three partners only in the firm, with clerical support, which will limit the number of contracts possible to be carried out each year to perhaps half a dozen. Any more would require additional staff.

3.1.4 Available finance is limited similarly, although given the award of contract there should be little problem in obtaining bank loans to cover operating costs.

3.2   Objectives

3.2.1 To secure contracts on the continent of Europe in addition to the UK business, which will increase your total revenue as follows:

Year 1985   increase of 20 per cent.
Year 1986   increase of a further 10 per cent.
Year 1987   increase of a further 10 per cent.

3.2.2 Profitability, measured as return on capital employed, to be increased:

Year 1985 – by 5 per cent if possible; but breakeven acceptable, allowing for initial costs and outgoings.
Year 1986 – by 5 per cent clear, after allowing for possible 1985 losses.
Year 1987 – by 15 per cent net return.

3.2.3 The target contract to be either a comprehensive operation covering the whole spectrum of the partners' expertise, or of a partial nature involving any of the individual partners' areas of specialisation.

3.3   Strategy

3.3.1 Selection of country. The three possibilities mentioned (3.1.2) are all 'big' in terms of potential numbers of possible clients. It is recommended, therefore, that one (France) be selected for initial research and then, if promising, for more extensive operations. If, after a period of six months, this country offers no prospects, then the exercise be repeated for Spain and then for Germany.

3.3.2 Notwithstanding this planned sequence, a watching brief should be maintained through the trade press and personal contacts, on the other two countries in case a particular opportunity arises. In any case, there could always be the possibility of a rolling development from one country to another. Although designs may differ between countries, the requirement for the service could be common and recommendations passed from one client to another.

3.3.3 Advertising and promotional activities should be put in hand (see Section C) and all inquiries followed up by post or phone as appropriate; and then by personal visit. Considerable importance is placed on the personal approach due to the nature of the business and the possible clients.

3.3.4 Given suitable interest by a client, initial designs and estimates could be prepared. It is essential at this stage to obtain the client's agreement on the actual work to be undertaken, the amount of money he or she is willing to spend and an agreement in respect of defraying costs and expenditure to date in the event of the client pulling out for any reason. Such estimates could always be modified subsequently by mutual agreement, but the costs incurred should be covered and made subject to stage payments as the work progresses.

3.3.5 While Interdecor's costs and fees can be calculated by the partners, the actual work to be carried out would, in all probability, have to be done by local contractors. Here the advice could be sought from the client, or from a local or national Chamber of Commerce or trade association. With local contract work, however, it would be essential to take legal advice, both from the point of the actual contract and also in respect of local labour law or conditions.

3.3.6 Depending on the nature and size of the contract, one of the partners should either be on site or pay periodic supervisory visits to ensure that the work is being carried out satisfactorily. Once a project is started, however, it should be possible for a partner to move on to the planning stage of the next project.

3.3.7 Both during the work on a contract and certainly on completion, every opportunity should be taken, locally and nationally in France and also in the UK, to publicize the work as outlined, in order to keep new work flowing in.

3.3.8 In the event of the planned approach to all three countries proving unremunerative within the 18 months, it is recommended that the partners should revert to UK operations while still keeping the foreign contacts open in case the situation improves.

4 Publicity and advertising in respect of overseas business

Note: As Interdecor is primarily a design service and as such mainly visual, illustrations will be an essential element in any promotional plans. To this end any material used should involve the best quality of photography and reproduction possible, laid out in the most tasteful ways to illustrate not only the quality of the actual work but also the company's skills in all relevant aspects of designing.

4.1 Before contacting any possible customers, it is essential that the firm should have a folio book of past work carried out, for instance on the stately home. This could include 'before' and 'after' illustrations, with suitable detail pictures and inscriptions to highlight particular or unusual features and treatments. It would also be advisable, if not recorded elsewhere, to include references to the colours, paints and fabrics used, together with the manufacturers or suppliers, so that immediate reference could be made to answer any queries.

4.2 This folio could also be reproduced in a sectional form, dealing with either a particular project completed or with common themes such as hotel or public rooms. These pamphlets could then be used for any relevant customer or as the basis for wider publicity. Apart from actual contracts completed, the opportunity could exist here for suitable stylized or conceptual designs which would show the designers' range of skills and abilities.

4.3 As the designing service is so individual, and particularly as the firm is likely to be completely unknown in the foreign market, it would be essential to include a descriptive insert of the three principals: their qualifications, experiences, particular areas of expertise and interest, together with such personal details as may be deemed appropriate or which might interest a particular client. Personal photographs could well be included.

4.4 Items mentioned in 4.2 and 4.3 could then be despatched on a selective basis at a rate of no more than six per month to the lists which had been compiled during the research phase. This controlled issue of material would be necessary to allow time for replies and specific following up which could arise. If several prospects replied, then subsequent mailings could be postponed until the earlier ones had been dealt with. Depending on the number to be sent, it is probable that at least £500 should be budgeted for this activity.

4.5 Direct advertising in French and English design magazines would be very expensive – even a modest insertion could cost £250–£500 per edition. However, it could be necessary to advertise in order to obtain what is likely to be far more effective, namely, an editor's interest in their presence and availability in France, so that the journal might be favourably inclined to include articles and features on the firm and its capabilities. Such publicity is more likely to attract notice than any other method.

4.6 One other aspect of publicity should be considered if the opportunity arises: to be present and participate in a suitable exhibition in France, perhaps an equivalent to the UK Ideal Homes. Such exhibitions are visited, among others, by individuals who could be considered as the target market and who would be on the look-out for new or appropriate ideas and approaches. Most exhibitions of this kind have press offices which not only supply details of exhibitions and their products or services but also are willing to give publicity to interesting exhibits. Again, BOTB assistance could be available to meet some of the costs involved in such activities.

7

CERTIFICATE IN MARKETING MINI CASES

Until now, the text has concentrated upon Diploma in Marketing mini cases. These are more difficult than certificate-level mini cases principally because they require more substantial answers. Students who have assimilated the information presented so far, should, therefore, find this chapter relatively 'easy'. This chapter has been deliberately placed here, rather than earlier in the text, because what has been written so far in relation to mini-case technique relates to *any* mini-case study. Had certificate-level cases been discussed and analysed at the beginning, we would have had to have introduced more narrative to explain how much more depth of analysis is required for diploma mini cases.

Mini cases were introduced into certificate-level examinations in June 1988 for the practice of marketing and practice of sales management papers with the objective of allowing students to demonstrate their understanding of the subject through the medium of a practical scenario. Thus, what the questioning seeks to achieve is knowledge of basic principles through an applied thought process. Questioning tends to address tactical problems rather than strategic issues. The dividing line between the approach to certificate as opposed to diploma mini cases is very thin, but we feel that it may be said that certificate questions are basically similar to the straightforward questions in Part B of each paper except that they must be answered through the medium of this scenario.

Initial observations from the senior examiners for these subjects suggest that many candidates are answering the questions set in a theoretical way, with very little recourse to the mini case itself. Clearly, candidates answering in this manner will score low marks because they have merely recited the theory and not demonstrated an understanding of what they have written through application.

The following mini cases are typical of those set in the practice of marketing paper and you will note that the questions set relate to practical issues. Answer them on your own, spending not more than one and a half hours on each and then examine the suggested answers.

PRACTICE OF MARKETING

Time allowed: 90 minutes

Provite

In just twelve months from now, the Orax Consumer Products Division of Orax pharmaceuticals plc is planning its biggest ever vitamin launch – that of Provite Effervescent Multivitamins.

Over the years, Orax has built a substantial business in the UK and European Community countries in ethical medicines. In more recent times, through the UK consumer division, Orax have established a significant market position in the £85m vitamins market.

The best known consumer vitamin product is Oradex, which is among the top five brands in the £8.5m vitamin C market. Until now, Orax does not have a branded entry in the multivitamins market sector, currently worth £45m, and growing rapidly.

With the tendency towards 'over the counter' medicines in pill and capsule form which are water soluble, Orax decided that Provite should have an effervescent formula. The launch of Provite in the UK was planned to build upon established consumer acceptance of effervescent vitamin products that are well established within the European Community and the USA.

Provite is to be a unique formulation of fourteen vitamins and nine minerals which, when dissolved in water, make up into a delicious citrus-flavoured fizzy drink.

Building upon substantial experience in pharmaceuticals marketing, Orax have enlisted the assistance of Charles Mason Associates to assist in the development stages up to the product launch.

Questions

1 You have been asked by Lenny Klein, marketing director of Orax Consumer Products Division, to explain the stages you would go through to design and implement a marketing research programme to assist with

the product positioning in the specified sector of the UK vitamins market.
2 Comment upon the dimensions of branding that are pertinent to the launch of Provite.

Answer to Question 1

Stages in the design and implementation of a marketing research programme for Provite

Stage 1: Basic problem conceptualization of marketing research brief

We would expect a client such as Orax to provide a clear brief which both explains the boundaries to the research programme and provides a clear sense of focus as to what is to be achieved.

It is important from the outset of such a project to be clear on the *purpose* of the research and the nature of the marketing decisions which are affected by the research findings.

Stage 2: Discussion with client

In relation to Provite we would need detailed discussions about the brief so that we understand clearly the parameters of the research and so that we both agree on the interpretation of the brief and the direction the research should take.

At this stage Orax Consumer Products Division could be of considerable help to declare the ad hoc research already considered and the availability of secondary sources within the department. This saves both time and client fees.

We would be interested also in your own beliefs about the products, its potential and the intended level of corporate commitment to it.

It is important to know how far Orax have gone with their launch plans. Is the research required to justify decisions already taken, or are the findings important to the development of a product launch plan? This will assist in the development of our research proposal and is not intended to be viewed as an item of importance.

Stage 3: Search related research

In the archives of Charles Mason Associates we will have reference to work completed on pharmaceuticals for previous clients plus a data bank relating to the industry.

It is our task to search our records to discover what we have on file and to consult external sources for research completed in the product field of over-the-counter non-prescription medicines with specific reference to vitamins.

Stage 4: Study the market and existing products

To become involved with the task it is important to have a feel for the product/market combinations. We will need to understand how the market is segmented, trends and buyer motivations, and to have an outline profile of competitive product offerings.

Stage 5: The proposal

Our proposal will be derived from your brief, our joint discussions plus our findings from the search we have conducted. This stage is critical. A marketing research exercise can only be as good as the proposal that has been agreed. In some cases clients are disappointed because the final report did not fulfil their expectations. The proposal will contain a clear statement of the research objectives to be achieved, the means by which the required information will be collected and when.

This written document must be the subject of close discussion so that both parties are quite clear on the precise task in hand. This avoids confusion, disappointment and frustration, and ensures that our time as consultants is effectively devoted to meeting client needs.

With our proposal you will find a covering letter outlining the basis upon which we work, with details of the level of fees and the means by which they are charged to you, our client.

Stage 6: The agreement

We require written confirmation of our proposal to finalize our contract and to agree the time scale for the project.

Stage 7: Internal resource planning

We have to 'book' your job and ensure that we have effective resource cover for the duration so that time deadlines are met. It will be our task to select the most appropriate team to handle Provite.

Stage 8: Information specification

Referring to our agreed proposal, we must now settle upon the precise interpretation of it by producing a comprehensive specification of the information needed to meet the objectives specified and agreed in the proposal. Again we will discuss and agree this with you, our client.

Stage 9: Survey design

9.1 *Analysis programme*
Having agreed the information requirements, the means by which this is achieved is of paramount importance.
   Therefore at an early stage in survey design we consider the form in which the analysis should be undertaken. This saves time at a later stage and may influence the data collection materials.

9.2 *Select survey methods*
The means by which the specified information is to be gathered is now decided from among a range of alternatives. The constraints of time and cost will influence the choice. It is of paramount importance that the methods selected are the most appropriate to obtain the data/information required.

9.3 *Sample selection*
Within the constraints of time and cost are the implications for accuracy and precision and the minimizing of bias in the results obtained.
   The technical area of sampling now has to be tackled in accordance with the above constraints. Above all we must ensure that the sample(s) selected are representative of the population from which they are drawn and appropriate to the research requirements.

Stage 10: Questionnaire design

To obtain the information specified it is often appropriate to design a formal questionnaire to be administered either by the respondent or by a trained interviewer. A great deal of skill is needed at this stage to ensure that all questions are relevant, are correctly sequenced to obtain the required response, and are designed to capture the precise information previously specified.

Stage 11: Pilot survey

Before the questionnaire is released on the sample of respondents previously determined it is important to test it out. Usually small changes are needed to obtain a clearer understanding of the questions for the respondent. Indeed, it may also be necessary to adjust the profile of the sample to obtain the desired results.

Stage 12: Appointment and briefing of interviewers

We usually subcontract all interview work to specialist field forces of trained interviewers. We find this is by far the best way to ensure professionalism for our clients. In the medical field, which is a specialist area, there are companies who provide first class service.

Jointly with our client we will brief the field supervisors, who each have a field force of interviewers whom they direct and control and subsequently brief on the nature of the research and the type of interview to be conducted and the way in which it should be effected.

The code of conduct of the Market Research Society is to be strictly adhered to.

Stage 13: The main survey

Following the briefing, at the agreed day the main survey will start for the time period specified to achieve the sample of respondents also agreed. Completed questionnaires will be returned to Charles Mason Associates. Our appointed field force will make random checks on all interviews to ensure that the integrity of the exercise is maintained.

Stage 14: Editing/coding of questionnaire

Some replies may require editing; others, where open ended questions are set, will require post coding. So a certain level of internal administration is needed before they can be passed for subsequent data processing.

Stage 15: Final tabulations and data processing

Before the analysis is run we check again with you, the client, on the form of the analysis to ensure that the analysis tables are tabulated to your needs. Once the data processing is completed, a computer print-out is received for our internal analysis.

Stage 16: Analysis, interpretation and report

The analysis and interpretation programme now relates back to our agreed proposal so that we then structure our findings according to the agreement between Orax Consumer Products Division and Charles Mason Associates on the previous information requirements for the project.

Our report is then structured to conform with the sections in the proposal, then presented to you together with the number of copies previously requested.

Answer to Question 2

Provite – dimensions of branding

Facts

1 Orax Pharmaceuticals plc are a significant force on the UK market for ethical pharmaceuticals and over-the-counter non-prescription medicines.
2 The branding of products is part of a conscious marketing policy.
3 They are established with Oradex in the vitamins market, but not in the multivitamins segment.
4 Of a total market of £8.5m the multivitamins sector, with a market value of £45m, represents a substantial opportunity for the launch of Provite with the source credibility of Orax Pharmaceuticals plc.
5 The product formulation should be well received and therefore potential brand associations should be favourable.

Branding

What makes a new brand successful? A million dollar question, but the answer may be 'becoming like an old one!'

We need to model the progress of established brands to better understand why they have been successful. Successful brands have something in their appeal which is 'just a little extra'. Oradex is among the top five brands in an £8.5m vitamin C market. Why? Because it has *added value*, a value actual or perceived in the mind of the consumer, which may fit well in the consumer's frame of reference and even take on different dimensions from those ever intended by Orax Consumer Products Division.

A successful brand such as Oradex appears to have balanced the key elements of product innovation, product quality and brand personality. Provite must aim to replicate this experience.

Most products in this field of over-the-counter non-prescription medicines are brought on the basis of repeat purchase arising from previous levels of product satisfaction.

The value of a new brand will nearly always depend upon past experience. Therefore the prime objective is to 'create trial' for this new multivitamin.

Consumers buy a 'bundle of satisfaction'. It may be the perceived fulfilment that will sway consumer preference for trial and then repeat purchase for Provite.

The source credibility of Orax Pharmaceuticals plc will give the support that the new brand will need in the early stages of its life cycle.

A successful brand has a number of both functional and non-functional appeals. It is the mix of both these ingredients that will influence consumer choice for Provite.

Dimensions of branding

1 Brand image

This is the personality of the product and must be congruent with the consumer's self image. The brand image for Provite must be built up through:

1.1 The brand name: which allows recognition and identity.
1.2 The pack: which allows immediate recognition through shape, design and the use of colour.
1.3 The promotion: which builds a platform for the virtues and associations which Orax need to convey to the trade and consumer.
1.4 The house style: which establishes credibility through an established range of Orax products.

2 Brand awareness

Creating rapid high levels of awareness can only be achieved through media advertising and then supported in stores by reminding consumers at the point of purchase.

Awareness levels can be 'tracked' throughout the life of the brand and provide an indication about the levels of media support required to maintain sales and market penetration.

3 Brand recall

Spontaneous recall has been achieved with a high percentage of consumers of vitamin C through the Orax product, Oradex. This takes time and a coincident investment in advertising and promotion. In time recall levels will be built for Provite.

4 Brand loyalty

Active support in continuing consumption of a particular brand in the face of competition by branded substitutes is the key to brand loyalty.

The role of advertising, which builds cognitive consistency, cannot be underestimated and should be of major concern in the launch of Provite.

The process of cognitive consistency will be endorsed through the reinforcement created by familiarization and usage of this brand of effervescent multivitamins. Confidence in the usage of Provite will build brand loyalty.

5 Brand perception

Consumer selective reception towards sensory stimuli, both conscious and unconscious, is a key element in brand perception. To achieve favourable brand perception for Provite, the appointed advertising agency must design messages for the brand that are consistent with consumers' needs, attitudes and cognitive systems so that the advertising message will pass through the consumers' selective perceptual filters.

Brand recognition

To assist the process of identification through the learning curve and associated memory recall, easily recognizable packaging and an easily remembered brand name are vital. Provite is a strong brand name with potential high impact. This must be balanced with appropriate pack design.

Brand symbolism

There are elements in the product's packaging such as shape, colour, design, material and labelling which provide the consumer with important information cues about the product.

Through this symbolism, the brand communicates meaning to consumers. Orax must ensure that the constructive elements of the brand, the unique selling points, carry the positive connotations associated with the consumer frame of reference.

For example, assuming that Provite will appear in tablet form, then, to add 'medical authenticity', it should appear in boxed form carrying clinical colours (e.g., blue and white or green and white). To create impact the brand name, Provite, must be bold, cited at the top of the pack, with a supportive Orax logo to build source credibility. A statement: 'Provite – Effervescent Multivitamins with Minerals', should appear in association with a medicine glass demonstrating the Provite tablet dissolving. The effervescence will be conveyed through bubbles rising from the tablet up towards the top of the glass. Dosage, contra-indicators and tablet ingredients clearly are needed to comply with legal requirements.

Brand positioning

The positioning of Provite can only be considered realistically from the consumer perspective.

It is the balancing of the marketing mix variables for the brand in the context of the competitive product provision in the multivitamin market sector which is the key to effective brand positioning.

It is often the more intangible dimensions of branding mentioned above that will establish a brand position for a product.

For Provite, it is vital to convey the benefits of the brand through media advertising, to create the threshold level of awareness beyond which consumers will actively search out the product. At this stage the positioning process will have started. The balanced combination of the marketing mix variables will then contribute to the successful launch of this new brand of effervescent multivitamins for the Orax Consumer Products Division of Orax Pharmaceuticals plc.

PRACTICE OF MARKETING

Time allowed: 90 minutes

Evans Instruments Ltd

Evans Instruments Ltd are a well-established British company based in Cambridge. The company has an international reputation built over the past sixty years on the manufacture and sale of a wide range of medical instruments for professional end use.

In more recent years Evans have produced a limited range of clinical health care products for sale direct to consumers through major multiple chemist outlets and pharmacies.

Currently in the development stage is a digital thermometer to be added to the existing range of products marketed to the general public.

The UK market for household thermometers is traditionally conservative and recent trade research indicates that less than 35% of households owned thermometers, of which 75 per cent were the conventional glass and mercury file type, a product with which Evans have supplied the medical profession for decades.

An independent survey conducted this year by Evans confirmed the trade research findings but also revealed that 90 per cent of those households owning a conventional thermometer considered it unsafe for young children. Glass is easy to break, potentially dangerous and the mercury inside is considered toxic.

Discussion groups revealed that it was difficult to establish if the temperature had been correctly taken and found the conventional type of thermometer difficult to read.

The research among non-owners revealed that over 50 per cent of respondents felt guilty for not owning a thermometer.

This research demonstrated a latent need for Evans' new product.

The Evans Digitherm is made from a durable, unbreakable, plastic polymer and gives an easily read digital display. The product is equipped with a self-timer with an audible signal to advise the user when the temperature is ready to be read. In short, the Evans Digitherm overcomes all the weaknesses associated with the conventional thermometer.

The plan now is to test market the product in London and the South East with regional TV support, but the marketing plans have yet to be finalized.

Evans have three competitors in this field who have launched similar products in the last 18 months, albeit with low profile marketing activity.

The product features vary, but fulfil the same function. They are selling currently in chemists and prices range from £7.95 to £11.95. Evans are concerned about the price level at which to enter the market and how to target the market for Digitherm.

Questions

1 Advise the consumer products division on how they could segment the market for Digitherm to define target markets.
2 How would you then advise Evans Instruments to proceed with setting the price for Digitherm?

Answer to Question 1

Market segmentation for Digitherm

A market is a place where buyers and sellers meet, where goods are offered for sale and where transfer of ownership takes place. A market may also be defined as the total demand for a given product. Fundamentally there are three factors to consider:

1 People with needs,
2 Their purchasing power,
3 Their behaviour.

From a practical viewpoint, to define a target market for Digitherm we must answer three questions:

1 Who are the buyers?
2 Where are they located?
3 What motives will induce purchase?

We will consider the process of market segmentation and make conclusions upon them for target markets.

Market segmentation for Digitherm

The process of market segmentation is to divide markets into meaningful buyer groups for the purposes of marketing to them on a focused and distinct basis.

It is now important to establish the bases for segmentation. Fundamentally there are two markets:

1 The trade market, comprising industrial buyers and their associated decision making unit.
2 The consumer market, comprising buyers with homogeneous characteristics.

The consumer market – bases for segmentation

Demographics

These are the most straightforward means by which markets can be delineated.

Age It is assumed that the market for Digitherm will be predominantly mothers, although there may be a secondary market among the elderly.

Sex It is thought that the purchase will normally be made by the female in her role as a mother, although among the elderly either sex may purchase.

Family life cycle Family units comprising mothers with children under five are considered the prime group.

Social class The market for this innovative product is considered to be ABC1.

Residential neighbourhoods While this may not be of direct relevance it is considered that the ACORN classification would apply and the following groups would be appropriate: modern family housing, higher incomes, older housing of intermediate status, affluent suburban housing.

Psychographics

Psychographic information is much more difficult to codify, but it does help to better discover *why* the product would be purchased. It is this area of purchase motivation which is so important for marketing communications planning.

It is considered that the following motivators would involve purchase for Digitherm:

1 Safety conscious mothers anxious about the hazards of using a conventional thermometer with young children.
2 Those concerned about the accuracy of the reading.
3 Those feeling guilty about non-ownership of a household thermometer.
4 Those realizing the need for and benefit of using a thermometer as a means to alert the household that someone is running a temperature.
5 Those concerned about justifying the need to call a doctor.

Geographics

At this stage the test market is London.

Conclusions on consumer market segmentation – target market definition

The primary market for the test is considered to be:

London-based, safety conscious, ABC1 mothers with children under five years of age who are anxious also about the hazards of using a conventional thermometer but who recognize the benefits of having one at home.

The trade market – bases for segmentation

The information provided indicates that the main retail outlets for Digitherm are major multiple chemists and pharmacies.

Size of firm/buying organization

This may be appropriate, because the larger companies such as major multiples would employ professional buyers, although independent pharmacies would depend upon the proprietor to make the purchase decision.

Buying situation

Because Digitherm is a totally new product not previously available, the buying situation is classified as a 'new buy'. As the product achieves market penetration among established outlets, the purchase becomes a routine rebuy.

In this new-buy situation there is a degree of perceived risk and therefore marketing tactics may be appropriate, particularly in the independent pharmacies, to reduce this risk.

Service elasticity

There may be a distinction between buyers on service levels, delivery times, and lead time on order turnaround, but for a new product such as Digitherm this may become inelastic as a direct function of media exposure and product promotion.

Price elasticity

The level of price sensitivity will be different throughout the retail outlet types and may be a function of buying power and the size of the organization. The company will be aware of this situation from existing trade relationships with buyers.

The decision making unit

In large purchasing organizations such as multiple retail chemists, a number of people may be involved in the overall purchasing process and influencing it, whereas in the case of the independent pharmacy this responsibility would rest with the proprietor or store manager. The implications for this are clearly for the selling and promotional methods which need to be applied.

Conclusions on trade market segmentation – target market definition

Two types of trade buyer emerge:

1 The DMU in the central purchasing function of multiple retail chemists making a new-buy decision.
2 The sole proprietor or store manager in an independent pharmacy also making a new-buy decision.

Answer to Question 2

Setting the price for Digitherm

There are a number of factors which need detailed consideration before setting the price for the first time for Digitherm.

External factors

The nature of market demand must be assessed. While the product features overcome the weaknesses of the conventional product and only 35 per cent of households own one, the research did not indicate the propensity to purchase.

Evans must determine if this product innovation *will* be adopted by consumers.

Furthermore, three competitors have already entered the market, so the Evans product merely follows the lead of competition where boundaries to the price range have been set.

Hygiene factors need consideration. Glass has been the traditional material because it is easily capable of being sterilized. Consumer perception of plastic polymer may be different and then coincidentally affect price perception.

With the technological advancement in digital technology, how long will it be before the established competitors launch an upgraded product, maybe with Centigrade and Fahrenheit displays, built-in memory features, etc.

Internal factors

Price can only be set in relation to a set of predetermined marketing objectives.

Evans Instruments are a well-known, creditable organization with close links to the medical profession. Diversification has occurred into clinical products for the household, and this is just another such item.

The bottom line is that if the product fails the company will survive. This places the product launch in perspective. Hence Digitherm could be viewed as an experimental product offering at this stage, the intention being merely to expand their current product range. Therefore market positioning must be considered.

The perception of the corporate identity of Evans may well be established and clearly any new products must trade upon the investment in this image over the years. Digitherm should not stand alone; it needs the brand support of 'another product from Evans Instruments Ltd – suppliers of medical instrumentation to the medical professions worldwide!'

This stance alone will condition the pricing decision. Price needs also to be assessed in relation to its interface with the other elements of the marketing mix. Selective distribution, an immature product and, one assumes, a relatively modest promotional stance, again have pricing implications.

Price setting methods

A number of dimensions must be considered.

1 The cost based approach:
  Using full absorption costing, a cost plus approach would be deemed appropriate, where fixed and variable costs equal total cost plus a percentage mark-up which equal the notional selling price. It implies that breakeven analysis and profit volume analysis would be used also to produce a target profit level for given sales of the product.

  This is a conventional approach and could be regarded as 'safe' and rational. However the company cannot lose sight of the boundaries set by competition.
2 The competition based approach:
  The range £7.95 to £11.95 gives a number of opportunities:

  (*a*) To undercut,

(*b*) To offer a mid-price, say, £9.95,
(*c*) To price the product at a premium of, say, £14.95.

The consumer will have an idea of the price that is appropriate for the product. Here again research would pay off.

> 'Would you buy Digitherm for your home?'
> 'How much would you be prepared to pay?'
> 'Are you aware of similar products?'
> 'What price do they currently charge?'

The price perception of the buyer should be tested.

The new product approach

Had Evans Instruments been the first to launch a digital thermometer then pricing for an innovative product would suggest skimming the market. The price levels have already been set by the innovators and the early adopters for the product have purchased. The diffusion process has begun and with it levels of price expectancy.

Product mix pricing

Perhaps a more realistic view is to consider the contribution that Digitherm will make to the current range of products offered by the company for the domestic household.

Established products have current price levels which may pose a lead to be followed. Indeed there may be complementary demand to consider where the trade-off will boost product profit contribution to the fixed costs of the company and the profitability of the consumer products division.

Pricing for trade channels

It is assumed that conventional trade channels will be used for Digitherm. Discount prices, trade allowances, quantity discounts, introductory offers – all have to be considered. Again this product may need to follow prevailing trade practices which Evans have established. The issue of seasonality cannot be ignored. Typically the 'cold and flu season' may well have a direct impact upon product sales.

It may be prevailing practice with trade channels to discriminate price by volume, by credit rating, by customer rating, by age of account and so on. There would seem little need to deviate from the established norms in this respect.

Psychological pricing

Competition have used 95p as a price point in the demonstrated price range from £7.95 to £11.95. The question to be raised is should this convention be followed for the Evans product, or should Digitherm be distinct at exactly the £ ceiling (i.e. £9.00, £8.00, £15) to push the product more up-market? The same effect could be achieved using 50p as a marker – £9.50, £14.50. The positioning strategy will give a good indication as to how to price the product from a psychological viewpoint.

Promotional pricing

Again depending upon the marketing objectives for the product which would give a clear sense of purpose for the Digitherm product strategy, the appropriateness of promotional pricing could be considered. However, considering the nature of the product and the nature of its innovative perception, this method of pricing is not deemed appropriate in the short term.

If competitors responded with new models, then would be the time to consider the future for the product and then would be the time to offer Digitherm as a loss leader. At this stage such considerations should be negated.

Geographic pricing

Should there prove to be an export market for Digitherm then the price levels should be adjusted accordingly.

For Evans Instruments to determine price levels and to proceed to agreement in this area then the above factors need to be given serious consideration before the pricing element of the marketing mix is agreed for Digitherm.

PRACTICE OF MARKETING

Time allowed: 90 minutes

Excel Power Supplies (EPS) Ltd

'With the sustained increasing use of computers and other sensitive electronic equipment in offices and factories, demand for uninterruptible and emergency power supplies appears endless,' claims Bryan Whitelock, Managing Director of Excel Power Supplies Ltd.

EPS, formed in 1969, recognized twenty years ago that power cuts and mains electricity variations such as voltage reductions and surges, spikes and frequency variations cause computer malfunctions, corrupt data transmissions and naturally in turn frustrate continuous systems control.

Today, EPS have established an acknowledged reputation as stand-by power specialists. Their USP is: 'We install and guarantee uninterruptible power supplies' – or for short, the EPS USP.

Their USP completely isolates sensitive electronic equipment from the incoming mains electricity and Excel claim that it is the only effective protection against all types of variation in the AC mains. Even the installation can be made with no break in the power supply during the change-over period of installation.

Excel Power Supplies carry a wide range of equipment to meet the demands of a wide variety of end-use applications so that they are in the total stand-by power business. Installations range from airports to hospitals, telecommunications to bakeries, from multinational corporations to independent companies, both within the UK, the Middle East and China.

Although sales are increasing with demand, so is competition. Bryan Whitelock recognizes the need to change from sales to marketing orientation. He claims: 'Our company's philosophy is to provide the highest quality products backed by excellent engineering and technical expertise.'

Questions

Bryan Whitelock is an electrical engineer, has had no formal business training, but has been made aware of the Chartered Institute of Marketing through members of his salesforce attending courses at the Institute's residential centre.

He realizes that it is time to develop a marketing planning system but currently has little knowledge about what is involved.

At this stage you have been asked to:

1 Advise Bryan Whitelock of certain key questions which should be raised and resolved before deciding to adopt a marketing planning system within Excel Power Supplies.
2 Identify clearly key benefits to be gained from the *process* of adopting a marketing planning system.

Excel Power Supplies Ltd

Introduction

Marketing plans may take a variety of forms ranging from verbal intentions to a set of budgets for achievement, through to formalized structures and procedures used as part of the corporate planning process. In many organizations in the commercial and non-commercial world they may not even exist.

By using a marketing planning approach marketing can become a better organized function and make a more substantial contribution to organizational performance in areas where marketing orientation is needed but has yet to be achieved.

Marketing planning must also be recognized as a management process – which means effective systems for organizing, directing, controlling, coordinating and evaluating cannot be ignored in the process of attaining profitable need satisfaction.

Answer to Question 1 – key questions to be raised

Like any planning system, the user must be clear on the intended use and the contribution desired.

Therefore, within Excel Power Supplies Ltd key questions must be asked:

1 Do we have the ability to match our ambitions? Often ambition to achieve a marketing planning system reaches beyond the realities of corporate capability.
2 Have we considered the planning horizons in terms of time?
3 Have we defined the boundaries to the system clearly?
4 What purposes are to be served by the marketing planning system?
5 What structure should exist to enable the plan to be implemented, planned and achieved?
6 What do we require to achieve the purpose we have now identified?
7 What constraints currently limit our ability to implement and can these be overcome?
8 What contributions are we seeking to organizational performance from the plan?

Like all planning, marketing planning concerns the future. It is the approach to the future which is important to be questioned.

Answer to Question 2 – benefits of a marketing planning approach

Marketing planning means *change*. It is a process of deciding currently what to do in the future with a full appreciation of the resource position, the need to set clear communicable, measureable objectives; the development of alternative courses of action and a means of assessing the best route towards the achievement of specified objectives. Marketing planning is designed to assist the process of marketing decision making under prevailing conditions of risk and uncertainty.

Above all the *process* of marketing planning has a number of benefits: The marketing planning process:

- Motivates staff.
- Secures participation and involvement.
- Achieves commitment.
- Leads ultimately to better decision making.
- Requires management staff collectively to make clear judgemental statements about assumptions – the very basis upon which the future depends.
- Ensures a systematic approach to the future has been taken.
- Prevents 'short termism', the tendency to place all effort on the 'here and now'.
- Creates a climate in which change can be made and in which standards for performance can be established.
- Enables a control system to be designed and established, whereby performance can be assessed against predetermined criteria.

Marketing plans can be both strategic and tactical, the latter operating within the framework imposed by the former.

Whether tactical or strategic, marketing planning requires the laying down of policies for the acquisition, use and disposal of resources.

Marketing planning as a functional area of planning activity can only work within a corporate planning framework. The marketing planner must not lose sight of the need to achieve corporate level objectives by means of exploiting product and market combinations. Therefore, there is an underlying requirement for any organization adopting marketing planning systems to set a clearly defined business mission as the basis from which organizational direction can develop.

Concluding comment

The questions to be raised and the benefits to be derived have been identified. However the transition from sales to marketing orientation will almost certainly involve change to the organizational culture.

Excel Power Supplies Ltd have enjoyed twenty years' trading by adopting sales orientation.

The incremental process of change to marketing orientation will cause tension within the company, uncertainty and even mistrust throughout the organization.

Full active commitment and support will be needed during the transition from Bryan Whitelock and his senior management team.

PRACTICE OF MARKETING

Time allowed: 90 minutes

Bodyfits

When the aerobics craze took the UK by storm in the early 1980s two Lancashire sisters, Sally and Linda French, took the opportunity to introduce 'Bodyfits' for the fit body.

'We could see that there would be a terrific demand for exercise wear and at that time women were looking for something more than T-shirts and shorts for their keep fit classes,' claims Sally French.

With initial capital of £40,000, the sisters rented factory space, bought the machines, hired a small team of workers and began production of Bodyfit leotards. By 1985 Bodyfits were supplying leotards to major department stores and exporting a small quantity to Scandinavia.

'At that time leotards were mainly available in black so we remembered the old Ford cliché and decided that it was high time to produce them in other colours too – that is when we really took off,' explains Linda French. 'The leotards sold like hot cakes so we hired a new designer and extended our range of Bodyfits to dance wear and accessories like waistbands, headbands and leg warmers.'

Today, the Bodyfits range has since expanded to include fashion wear – all designed with fun and practicality in mind.

Sally further explains that Bodyfits clothing uses nylon, lycra, cotton and various combinations of each for their garments so that the clothing returns to its original shape after stretching, fits like a second skin and is absorbent to keep the body cool.

Factory space has been extended. Fifty employees are now engaged producing 3000 dozen clothing pieces per month.

So what is the secret of Bodyfits' success?

Linda states: 'Our quality is similar to imported brands. We work on slim margins to be price competitive but we offer more colours and a wide range of styles. Now we accept designs from freelancers who are in touch with the market. Also people nowadays are really health conscious and are into all kinds of exercise programmes – there is just so much potential.'

Question

The Lancashire sisters are, however, wise enough to realize that their good fortune may not last for ever without a more formal system of marketing planning and control.

You have been asked to draft a report to explain the essential elements of a marketing plan. The report would then be used as the basis for subsequent discussions within the company as a means of achieving sustained growth and profitability.

A marketing plan for Bodyfits

Introduction

To date the success of the business has been led by very favourable market demand and hence the company has been carried along with this market surge.

A marketing plan and the system for achieving it demands a more disciplined approach to planning than has previously occurred.

This report outlines (*1*) the essential elements of the plan (*2*) and gives a brief explanation of each section so that may provide the basis for further discussion.

Part 1 – essential elements for a typical marketing plan

1 The corporate plan remit.

    1.1 The corporate mission.
    1.2 Corporate objectives.
    1.3 Corporate constraints.

2 The marketing audit.
3 SWOT analysis.
4 Assumptions.
5 Time scales.
6 Marketing objectives.
7 Marketing strategies.
8 Marketing tactics.
9 Selling and sales management.
10 Staffing the plan.

11 Contingency measures.
12 Review, control and budgets.

Part 2 – explanation of the sections outlined in part 1

1 *The corporate plan remit*

1.1 *The corporate mission*

The corporate mission statement needs detailed consideration by Sally and Linda to establish the business the company is really in and relate this consideration to future business intentions.

The statement is a general statement that provides an integrating function for the business, from which a clear sense of business definition and direction can be achieved.

This stage is often overlooked in marketing planning and yet without it the plan will lack a sense of contribution to the development of the total business as a whole. By deriving a clear mission statement, boundaries for the business can be conceived in the context of environmental trends that influence it.

It is helpful to establish the areas of distinctive competence and, in so doing, focus upon that which customers are buying rather than upon what the company is selling. This will assist in the development of a more marketing orientated mission statement; therefore take into account trends in market consumption patterns. A clear mission statement should include the customer groups to be served, the customer needs to be served and the technologies to be utilized.

1.2 *Corporate objectives*

The corporate objectives of the organization are time dependent and determined to achieve shareholder expectations. These should be derived from the mission statement to ensure integration within a corporate and marketing planning system.

The time horizon will vary from organization to organization, from market to market and country to country, time-scales stretching from one to five – even to twenty years. In Bodyfits' business, with the demands of changing fashions, the time-scale is likely to be shorter than for many organizations.

From a practical viewpoint both quantitative and qualitative objectives are required to provide the foundation upon which measureable marketing activities can be planned for.

In particular, quantitative corporate objectives concerned with rates of return on capital employed and invested, return on shareholder funds, etc.

are inextricably linked to the company's financial year where these key ratios are used as indicators of annual financial performance.

Qualitative corporate objectives may relate to image, stance, positioning, projection, appeal, identity and recognition. These you appear to be well aware of.

Essentially objectives are statements of *what* is to be achieved and hence provide the stimulus for strategy, i.e., the means by which the objectives will be achieved.

Because these objectives are corporate and thus have company-wide parameters, balance is a keyword for the attainment of integration of the organization as a whole.

Areas to consider when setting corporate level objectives include:

- Market standing.
- Innovation.
- Productivity.
- Physical and financial resources.
- Staff performance, development and attitude.
- Public responsibility and profitability.

1.3 *Corporate constraints*

It is the matching of ambition to ability to maximize performance that is the perennial task which besets senior management of most organizations. Bodyfits is no different.

Corporate constraints, therefore, are the limiting factors which govern corporate capability.

Again, a useful classification here is to consider a matrix as shown below:

	Quantitative	*Qualitative*
Internal		
External		

As the process of planning is iterative, a clearer understanding of these constraints may arise at subsequent stages in the planning process.

A full appreciation of corporate capability at this stage will effect more realistic resource deployment at later stages in the marketing plan and also assist the cross-functional plans which collectively are designed to achieve corporate level objectives.

2 *The marketing audit*

In most business enterprises, periodic financial reviews are mandatory and systems are established to ensure that these occur within the time deadlines set. This should be the case with marketing but rarely is it so formalized.

Essentially the marketing audit is a systematic internal and external environmental review of the company's marketing performance for a given period of time. This review provides the basis for subsequent SWOT analysis (see section 3).

The purpose of auditing the external and internal environment of the organization is to separate controllable from uncontrollable variables which have a significant impact on corporate performance. Companies should develop a customized checklist of factors for examination which can then be reviewed systematically and periodically.

The external audit will examine the PEST factors – political, economic, social and technological – in the general business environment, and consider the fiscal and legal impact of these on company operations. In addition, a comprehensive market profile is required with a detailed understanding of market movements so that forecasts can be developed for market performance and changes thereto. To support this market profile, the company must place itself in the context of a competitive market environment and a comprehensive profile of competition must be obtained, together with an examination of competitive product offerings.

Internally, a thorough examination of the company's marketing performance is vital. Detailed sales analysis, market shares and profit contribution analysis must be undertaken together with an assessment of the efficiency of the company's marketing mix and marketing control plans and procedures.

The process of auditing will raise a series of questions and will produce a series of discoveries. These will need to be compiled into an acceptable format for presentation, a format from which later stages of the plan can be developed. This format is known as 'SWOT analysis'.

3 *SWOT analysis*

The mnemonic classifies the results of the audit into internal current strengths and weaknesses which largely concern controllable variables and external future opportunities and threats which concern largely uncontrollable variables.

It should be emphasized that the SWOT analysis used for presentation should be a succinct summary of the audit which concentrates upon main issues for resolution and for which objectives, strategies and tactics could be set if so required.

4 *Assumptions*

In order to move forward from analysis into planning, a conceptual transition is now required because something has to be achieved from that which has been assessed, discovered and recorded.

The environmental scanning of the market, the analysis of the competitive and market situations lead naturally to the statement of assumptions for a future planning time horizon. Without stating assumptions, we must have perfect knowledge – this is rare. It is upon the statement of assumptions that progress can now be made to the planning stage. Assumptions can be classified as internal and external; quantitative and qualitative in the same format as previously prescribed for corporate constraints.

5 *Time-scales*

It is normal practice to design an annual marketing plan which coordinates with the fiscal year of the organization and hence integrates with the budgetary control and associated management information and control systems. Some companies then extend the planning horizon to a separate plan for five years, or incrementally to five years on a rolling planning basis. It is wise to apply a rolling planning principle so that plans are always at least one year ahead, although revised and updated quarterly.

6 *Marketing objectives*

To restate a point made earlier, objectives are statements of *what* is to be achieved, and strategies are the *means* of achieving objectives. The two should not be confused.

It is of considerable importance to realize that marketing objectives should be derived directly from corporate level objectives and, in turn, reflect both quantitative and qualitative areas.

Concentration should be focused on setting objectives for products and markets because corporate level objectives reflect product/market combinations. Marketing mix objectives can be separated out at a later stage.

This simplifies the process of setting marketing objectives but, remember, they must be actionable, achievable and measureable – otherwise the accomplishment of marketing strategies cannot be accurately assessed of the prescribed time scale of the plan.

7 *Marketing strategies*

Strategy is the means by which objectives are achieved. If objectives specify *what* is to be done, then strategy lays down *how* it is to be done.

Determined strategy then leads to a series of action statements which are a clear set of steps to be followed to achieve the determined strategy. These actions are known as tactics.

Effective marketing strategy is critical to the success of the plan. It must exploit the strengths and opportunities, overcome weaknesses and avoid threats identified in the SWOT analysis.

A strategic marketing programme depends upon an incisive SWOT analysis and arising from that clear market definition of planned marketing activity, company success is governed by marketing strategy. A company's marketing strategy is the very basis upon which operational decisions are made and corporate/marketing objectives achieved within the time periods specified for the plan. The time period for the tactical plan is usually one year – the current operating year. It is through the tactical plan that marketing strategy is achieved in practice.

Commonly, the strategic element of the marketing plan concentrates upon the four Ps of product, price, promotion and place, but these could be extended to cover the wider reaches of the marketing spectrum often required in planning frameworks.

It is suggested that market and marketing research is not overlooked since information provides a vital strategic contribution to the plan.

A key element of the strategic elements of the marketing plan, again often overlooked, is the policy statement which provides the guidelines by which the four Ps can be accomplished within the determined time planning horizons.

As part of strategic determination, it is common practice to identify alternative means by which specified marketing objectives can be achieved, then set criteria for evaluation, apply these to the stated alternatives and select the best course of action.

The intention of marketing mix strategy is to achieve market positioning for product/market combinations specified in the corporate and marketing objectives sectors above. Therefore, market definition, market segmentation and market targeting are the prerequisites within which positioning must be achieved.

8 *Marketing tactics*

The level of marketing strategy will vary from plan to plan, company to company, but the final intention is to put the plan into action. It is now time to construct a set of detailed action programmes to achieve the

previously stated marketing strategy. The level of the tactical plan is who
should do what, where, when, how and why. In this way responsibility,
accountability and action over a one-year time scale can be planned,
scheduled, implemented and reviewed. This section could be headed
programming, but this introduces another term which is not particularly
helpful – the emphasis however is upon actions to be taken.

9 *Selling and sales management*

In many companies, the sales plan will be separated from the marketing
plan or, indeed, will replace the marketing plan in a sales orientated
situation.

However, if we adopt marketing as a business philosophy then sales
must be included within the marketing plan – it is the means by which many
of the plan's objectives will be achieved. Sales forecasts and budgets will
provide the means for quantitative achievement and control.

Selling and sales management strategy and tactics should be designed to
complement, support and integrate with the marketing mix components of
marketing strategy – in particular promotion and distribution.

10 *Staffing the plan*

Objectives and strategy can only be achieved through people, structures,
systems and methods.

In the tactical section of the plan, responsibility and authority for
operations should be designated. However, a total consideration is
required for organizational and manpower development – to bring about
the changes required to meet the plan's objectives.

Training and development, career development programmes, remuneration systems, headcount, etc. need to be considered and, usually, will
require liaison with the personnel function.

11 *Contingency measures*

Despite planning ahead for change, environmental factors often force us to
change our course of action – often these factors are unforeseeable and
frustrating. The time taken to adjust may be less rapid than we would like
in order to avoid higher costs and incurring losses. Under such conditions
response to contingency situations becomes reactive. To minimize the
impact of changed environmental circumstances, companies can be
proactive by using contingency thinking to anticipate likely events which
may occur, and then make plans to reconcile the changed position in which
the company may then be placed.

For each element of marketing mix and sales strategy, the marketing planner should ask the question 'what if?'. In so doing, a change scenario will be formulated, a scenario to which the company can now choose to respond.

By planning ahead, the impact of changes will be reduced. Such thinking when used in marketing planning, also encourages control and may prevent the cost of expensive mistakes.

12 *Review, control and budgets*

A marketing plan cannot be operated without a control environment to monitor and measure progress.

A system of controls should be laid down whereby the plan is reviewed on a regular and systematic basis, and then updated to extend the horizon to the prescribed time scale.

Controls are needed to assess tactics and strategy in the progress towards the achievement of quantitative and qualitative objectives. Therefore, controls should be seen as both quantitative and qualitative in design.

The marketing information system and management information system provide essential inputs to the control system, but we depend upon people to work the system through regular appraisal.

Comparison of performance against target and the coincident variance analysis will enable corrective action to be taken to further exploit marketing and market opportunities and threats.

Again, contingency planning is a form of control that can and should be used, particularly where markets are volatile.

To some marketing personnel, marketing budgets alone are marketing plans in that they forecast projected income and expenditure for a given period of time, but for companies using a formalized system of marketing planning, the budget is the means by which the entire plan is coordinated financially.

Each area of marketing activity should be costed and then allocated to centres of responsibility. Indeed, as a key functional area of business the marketing budget is one of the key budgets to contribute towards the total budgetary control system of the organization.

In many organizations, budgeting is the transitional step between planning and implementation because the budget, and allocated centres within it, will project the cost of each activity over the specified period of time and, also, act as a guide for implementation and control.

Conclusion

The demands of a marketing planning system are considerable. This document will require detailed reflection upon the way the business is currently run and how it should now be managed to achieve future growth and profitability.

After having examined the suggested solutions you will quickly realize that it is not physically possible to write this amount in one and a half hours. Expanded solutions have been given in order for you to ascertain whether or not your solutions have incorporated *some* of the ideas and structures that we have suggested.

There now follows two practice of sales management mini-case studies and suggested solutions. The first (International Mutual Limited) was taken from the June 1988 sitting. The second (Associated Volvex plc) is a 'typical' mini case.

PRACTICE OF SALES MANAGEMENT

Time allowed: 90 minutes

International Mutual Limited

Although the company's roots can be traced back to Chicago in the 1920s, International Mutual have only been trading in the United Kingdom since 1973. Most insurance companies tend to cover a broad spectrum of insurance services like automobile, fire, life, etc. International Mutual concentrates on the personal health and personal accident fields.

Their growth can best be measured by the increase in the volumes of premiums collected in a financial year, and some of their annual volumes have been as follows:

	1972	1975	1978	1981	1984	1987
£ million	2.1	7.2	11.6	21.7	24.6	27.2

During this time, the rate of sales of new business has steadily increased, but this was accompanied by a disturbing increase in the cancellations of existing policies.

The task of the sales person is divided into three parts:

1 Gaining new business.
2 Servicing existing policies (i.e., renewing them).
3 Upgrading existing policies (i.e., persuading customers to increase their cover).

The company does not advertise and rotates its coverage of territories on a six monthly basis. Thus, customers see a representative only twice a year.

For the sales manager there are persistent problems. Staff turnover is high with the average length of employment of the sales person being six months. His success, therefore, depends upon having a 'core' of long-serving members in his sales team.

New members of the sales team take some time to become useful and productive employees. Once hired they spend two weeks in a training school to learn the standard sales presentation, how to answer objections and some knowledge of consumer and organizational buying behaviour.

The marketplace primarily consists of shops and other small businesses.

In addition, the more enterprising sales people endeavour to sell to larger businesses and through bank managers, solicitors and accountants. Cold calling on individual homes also features when attempting to find business.

Commission is earned both on sales and upgrades and also by renewing and collecting premiums on existing policies. A problem for the sales manager is in motivating the sales force to spend as much time and energy in gaining new business as the energy they seem to spend in servicing the old.

The sales manager's job in fact depends upon producing an increase in premium volume in each six-monthly cycle. That, in turn, depends upon his ability on a number of fronts:

(a) Selecting the right people for training.
(b) Early field training in order that sales people can quickly apply what they have learned in training.
(c) Retaining a core of successful sales people and motivating them to continue their success.
(d) Ensuring that sufficient time is left to go on selling missions with his sales staff, as well as selling on his own account.

Questions

1 Advise the sales manager upon International Mutual's commission structure. Does it encourage the retention of good sales people?
2 'The training of sales people should not be limited to their induction into the company, but should be an on-going process.' Discuss this contention in relation to this situation.

Answer to Question 1

1 *Introduction*

The total remuneration package offered to sales people may consist of a number of component parts:
(a) Basic salary.
(b) Commission/bonus.
(c) Car or car allowance.
(d) Expenses and other personal allowances, e.g. clothing allowance, preferential loans or low rates of interest, etc.
The ratio of basic salary to total potential earnings differs between industries and even among different firms in the same industry.

2 *Current practice*

(*a*) It is common practice within the insurance business that sales people are paid on a commission system only, with no basic salary or car/car allowance. Hence sales people are, to all intents and purposes, self-employed and paid *only* on results. If they do not manage to sell a policy or upgrade an existing policy holder they receive no payment whatsoever.

(*b*) The philosophy behind such a commission structure is to keep the sales force on its toes and 'hungry' for success. The commission system is designed to ensure that individual sales people view sales success as an absolute necessity because, basically, if they do not sell they do not get any money to live, pay their mortgage, buy petrol, etc. The prospect of being without money to live on concentrates the mind wonderfully and acts as a strong propellant to increase effort. The stimulus to effort is basically fear; fear of failure and insecurity.

3 *Implications*

(*a*) While such a philosophy works in the short term, its long-term effects are open to question.

(*b*) International Mutual has problems retaining sales personnel beyond an average employment time of six months.

(*c*) Even the best sales people owe it to themselves and their families to secure their futures. A commission-only occupation is an extremely precarious way of earning a living.

(*d*) A realistic basic salary would remove some of the pressure of insecurity, create a feeling of belonging to the firm and may well contribute to more good sales people remaining with International Mutual for longer periods.

(*e*) Sales personnel are failing to get a sufficient amount of new business. Because the commission structure means they have to sell to live, it is probably perceived as being easier to make a secure income from servicing existing clients and getting repeat business or upgrading policies than attempting to gain new business.

(*f*) Servicing existing clients is of paramount importance in retaining and repeating business, but new business is necessary to offset cancellations and achieve constant growth (i.e., the sales manager's job depends upon producing an increase in premium volume in each six monthly cycle).

(*g*) The best sales personnel are usually those with the most adept sales skills and who are capable of prospecting and generating new business.

4 *Recommendations*

(a) A differential rate of commission (i.e., a higher rate than repeat business or upgrading) on new business will encourage the better sales people to spend more of their time prospecting.

(b) The extra financial rewards resulting from the above will give better staff an additional goal to aim for as well as presenting them with a more challenging job. It will also act as an incentive for such staff to stay with the company.

(c) Training schemes should be devised to explain to new sales people that it is better to build up a solid customer base, because repeat business will bring greater potential rewards in the longer term.

Answer to Question 2

1 *Introduction*

Induction training is an absolute necessity when a new recruit joins the sales team. Induction training should ideally include such things as:

(a) Product knowledge (including price).
(b) Company knowledge.
(c) Knowledge of systems and procedures.
(d) Selling processes and techniques.
(e) Knowledge of competitors.

2 *Current situation and implications*

2.1 New members of the sales team take some time to become useful and productive employees. Once hired, they spend two weeks in a training school to learn:

(a) Standard sales presentations,
(b) How to answer objections,
(c) Some knowledge of consumer and organizational buying behaviour.

2.2 This initial training session is the first and only programme of instruction in the whole of the sales person's career with the company. There is a great danger in viewing training as a necessary evil that needs to be dealt with as soon as possible, and as something that once it is over it is finished with. This view is myopic, to say the least, not to say naive and simplistic. Obviously the management of International Mutual do not appreciate the concept that success comes through people. Training is not a 'one-off' thing to be 'got out of the way' but should be a continual process of personal achievement and adaptation to changing circumstances.

2.3 New sales recruits are given induction training in standard sales presentation techniques, but new techniques are being developed and circumstances change. New conditions in the external business environment may necessitate the use of a different approach and a different (not necessarily new) set of 'techniques'.

2.4 Customers need and want change in response to environmental changes. Different business conditions, adverse economic climate or other environmental change may give rise to different customer priorities, different reasons for purchasing or not purchasing and different reasons for objecting. A 'potted' course in the first two weeks is highly unlikely to equip the modern professional sales person with the knowledge and skills he or she will need throughout an entire career.

2.5 A final point relates to International Mutual's high rate of staff turnover. Professional sales people want a career not just a job. Many employees perceive regular training as a valuable thing. It assists them in both personal development, job satisfaction and in obtaining promotion. Often posts without training are viewed as 'dead-end jobs' with no career path or scope for personal development. Introducing an on-going programme of regular updating training sessions may well contribute to retaining a higher proportion of good staff.

3 Conclusion

Success comes through people. Training is not a 'one-off' expense to get out of the way as soon as possible; rather it is an investment in human capital. Customer needs and wants and the general external environment are in a constant state of change. A one-off induction course at the start of a sales person's career with the company is inadequate. Training should be a regular, systematic and on-going process. Regular training results in a more adept and efficient sales team, a chance of personal development and hence greater overall job satisfaction and sales performance.

PRACTICE OF SALES MANAGEMENT
Time allowed: 90 minutes

Associated Volvex plc

Associated Volvex is a British company established in 1937 to supply fittings for the furniture trade. Then, it employed just twelve shop-floor personnel, one secretary, an accounts clerk and the manager who also performed a selling role. Throughout the past fifty years the company has seen many changes and it has grown to its present size where it employs 12,000 people in seven different countries.

The company has three main manufacturing divisions in the UK as follows:

1 *Volvex Fibreline.* This division produces cellular foams and fibres, primarily as filling materials and textiles for the clothing industry.
2 *Volvex Extrudaline.* This division produces extruded plastics for such applications as window gasket seals, uPVC window frames and industrial seals.
3 *Volvex Resinline.* This division produces polymers in the form of pellets as a raw material for plastic extrusion.

Andrew Vickers is the UK General Sales Manager for Associated Volvex plc. (AV) Until one year ago, he was with another company that was involved solely in the manufacture and sale of polymer resin pellets. Since coming to AV he has been 'thrown in at the deep end' with two products with which he was not familiar in the technical sense. Vickers reports to the Sales and Marketing Director, Nigel Horne, who, despite his title, is primarily a market researcher. Horne has little practical experience of sales, but has laid down 'rules' of how the sales side of the business is to be run.

It is Horne's view (with board approval) that an integrated sales force should have responsibility over all the products sold within the group. In terms of technology and technical understanding, there is a common thread, but groupings of customers are totally diverse. The emphasis on sales, therefore, is different for each product group. To explain:

Fibreline

Textiles, such as acrylics, polyester and nylon are sold direct to textile mills. These tend to be concentrated in areas like West Yorkshire, Lancashire and the East Midlands. By contrast cellular foams are sold principally to two bedding manufacturers and one volume furniture manufacturer. Smaller manufacturers tend to buy from factors and wholesalers who are scattered all over the country. Such distributors are thus AV representatives' target customers.

Extrudaline

Extruded plastic products can be produced in several different materials in a variety of intricate profiles. This is the high technology side of AV's business. Where the customer is in the chemical engineering business, there is often a need to know the properties of materials and profiles under specific conditions of temperature, pressure, acidity and alkalinity. They may need to be resistant to solvents and even to abrasives. Sales are principally direct to customers rather than through factors.

Resinline

Any company dealing in plastic forming and extrusion uses polymers in pellet form as its basic raw material. The choice of material is often accompanied by a specification that demands conditions of hygiene in manufacture and resistance to chemical attack.

Customers vary enormously in size, the largest buying in huge bulk from AV and the smallest from AV distributors. What most customers require is specific advice on material specification. Customers are located randomly throughout the UK.

Vickers has asked Horne to analyse sales for the past three years by sales representative, by market type and by geographical area. Horne has personally compiled a report which assesses the number of factors and distributors, end users and possible key accounts. It has been on Vickers' mind to compare the two documents and use the findings to compile a sales strategy for the next three years.

It is known that sales have been growing slowly over the past three years, but there is no effective yardstick as to relative performance relating to the market as a whole. Although AV is the overall market leader, several smaller companies are known to be undergoing rapid expansion programmes.

All plastic products are oil based. This means that sterling/US dollar exchange rates are crucial to the profitability of the company as oil is always purchased in US currency. Up to now this has been to AV's advantage because its size makes it cost effective to have a long-range economic planning facility. Recently, however, this reliance on exchange rate forecasting has been questioned. Exchange rates fluctuate with less certainty than before and high interest rates mean that stock levels are critical. This has led the board to commission a study on 'just-in-time' (JIT) manufacturing.

As the name implies, JIT means that a bare minimum of stocks are carried both of finished products and of raw materials, with a view to saving on the costs of stockholding. This means that the sales force must be fully aware of lead times in manufacture and only the fastest moving lines can now be supplied ex-stock.

This is causing Vickers some concern as there is little turnover of staff in the field sales force (the average length of time with AV being over ten years). They have been used to dealing with customers in a set way which has included the provision of an ex-stock delivery service.

The company has just installed a statistical process control system over their manufacturing processes. They have, in addition, been awarded the quality certificate BS 5750: Part 2 over all three product ranges. Vickers has received feedback from the sales force that this is a very welcome development. Arising from these developments, Vickers hopes to introduce a number of changes with as little conflict as possible.

Sales representatives in AV are presently given targets and commission which relate directly to their previous achievements. These do not refer particularly to product mix, but only to sales revenue.

A comparison of Horne's marketing report with an analysis of sales has revealed two things:

1 Out of six sales representatives, two are responsible for 80 per cent of Extrudaline products. These two do not operate in geographical areas which suggest that this should happen.
2 Three out of the other four representatives make almost all of their sales in the textile and cellular foam market. The fourth seems to concentrate on the resin pellet market. This seems to go against the assessed market opportunities.

Questions

1 Vickers inherited an organization which based its sales force structure on proximity of the sales force. Prepare a report to management that:
(a) Comments upon the logic of this strategy. (*10 marks*)
(b) Discusses alternative strategies. (*30 marks*)

(c) Makes recommendations for any change you believe might be necessary. (*10 marks*)   (*Total 50 marks*)
2 Comment upon the training and motivation of the sales force, making any recommendations that would help to solve any problems that may exist. (*50 marks*)

Answer to Question 1

1(a) *Sales force organization*

For optimum results, it must follow that an optimal sales force structure should be in place. Variables which influence the sales force structure are as follows:

(*i*) The breadth of the company's product line. How technologically related are the products? Can they all be readily understood by the same person?

(*ii*) The number and type of market segments served. How senior in the organization do the buyers tend to be? Is supplier selection a strategic or tactical issue in the markets served? Is it a 'one off' decision, followed by repeat orders, or is close liaison necessary? Is price, delivery time or some other factor going to be the deciding factor for selling?

(*iii*) The size and financial resources of the manufacturer. Is the number of field sales representatives kept to an absolute minimum? Does on-going sales training feature strongly?

It can thus be seen that the present strategy has not been clearly thought through and has probably evolved from small beginnings. The present structure is thus there more by accident than by design.

1(b) *Alternative strategies*

Strategy 1: Organization by product type

To describe this kind of organization, it is best to envisage a company whose products are technically diverse, yet where there is a relatively large number of such products. In such circumstances, there would tend to be a relatively small number of accounts for each product, yet each would need a relatively large amount of technical support.

Where products vary in their relative technical complexity, patterns of purchasing behaviour are also likely to vary. A repeat order will normally be handled by a buyer without recourse to other authority. By contrast, items of capital equipment are normally purchased after management approval. The level of management approval necessary does vary from company to company, but it is safe to say that such expenditure is approved by technical and/or financial people.

For technical consumables, although these are purchased as repeat orders, purchasing policy often changes. The customer has technical constraints that change according to end-user requirements. For this reason, policy can often be influenced by a technically orientated sales person.

Advantages

(*i*) Development of specialist technical knowledge by each representative.
(*ii*) Identification of new technical market segments by close cooperation with customers.
(*iii*) Typing-in of customers to the company by dependence on jointly developed products.

Disadvantages

(*i*) High cost – both of specialized training and of prolonged sales visits to fewer customers.
(*ii*) Need to justify sales expenditure on a product-by-product and customer-by-customer basis.
(*iii*) Close cooperation may lead to product development that is too specialized to have a market elsewhere. Profit opportunities may thus be severely restricted.

Strategy 2: Organization by geographical area

This is a common strategy in that it is simple to organize. The sales representative covers a specific territory.

For non-technical markets this is the most cost-effective option. Not only are expenses kept down, but time is optimized and journey planning becomes a routine operation. Sound relationships can develop around such routine visits.

This is how the company is organized at present, treating the market in any area as a homogeneous whole.

Advantages

(*i*) Lower unit selling costs due to savings in time and logistics,
(*ii*) Regular visits creating a routine (representatives are expected),
(*iii*) Relatively good understanding between representatives and clients.

Disadvantages

(*i*) A tendency for the representatives to be a generalist which can lead to lack of technical knowledge,

(*ii*) There can be a lack of control by management over product lines in that specialization is down to individual representatives,

(*iii*) There can be a tendency for salespeople who are not totally familiar with the product to bargain a price owing to an insufficient appreciation of the product and its applications and its true value to the customer.

Strategy 3: Organization by market segment (customer type)

There are parallels to organization by product type, but the difference here would not be on what product is consumed by the customer, but what product is produced by the customer. Firms producing electronic goods are likely to use the same products. Technological changes are, therefore, likely to come about due to a change in industry practices which must affect consumption. Understanding of a customer's market must also convey knowledge to likely changes in the market as it affects the producer.

In addition, the purchasing structures of like organizations are likely to bear similarities and so ease the path of sales representatives with experience of those industries.

1(c) *Recommendations*

It is evident that a geographical organization is not serving the company particularly well. Extrudaline products, for example, are being sold effectively in only two out of the six territories. This product falls into a 'technical consumables' category. There is also an inference that no particular attention is being paid to the Resinline group of products.

Recommendations centre upon which emphasis to place on alternatives to the present situation. In practical terms, there may be little difference between a product centred approach and a market centred approach. The former may lead to greater technological advances, but these may not lead to greater sales or profits. It is evident that this is the way in which sales representatives are operating at present. To encourage them to do so on a wider geographical front can only lead to increased sales. However, this may not halt the apparent neglect of the Resinline series of products.

A market-led approach must inevitably look towards capacity and trends in each market. Rather than concentrate upon a link-up with specific manufacturers, it should be possible to concentrate upon the benefits that particular groups of manufacturers are likely to be seeking. Added value will thus be achieved from volumes sold of current products. These profits can then be channelled into technologically advanced projects to achieve a long-term benefit.

Answer to Question 2

1 *Training of the sales force*

To be effective, a sales person needs to possess several skills simultaneously. These can be categorized in a number of ways:

(*a*) Product related skills, i.e., knowledge of the product and its associated applications plus knowledge of the company.
(*b*) Communications skills, i.e., the ability to speak in a way which is clearly understood and be able to write concisely upon specific situations.
(*c*) Empathy – or the skill of expressing common cause. Even when inwardly disagreeing with views expressed by another party it is important to understand the other viewpoint.

Training has two functions:

(*i*) It allows the company's management to impart policy to those dealing with customers.
(*ii*) It enables management to assess where further support or training is necessary.

Firms periodically change their marketing and financial strategies. Training programmes enable them to impart their views to the sales force. A market segmentation strategy is worked out by marketers, but it is physically put into operation by the sales force. Only on-going training will enable this to be carried out effectively.

A further benefit of sales training is continuity. Selling, in essence, is an isolated task, in which the individual is often left to make decisions without recourse to anything except precedent. Training courses 'bind' together a sales force in ways that meetings cannot. Frank exchanges of view are more likely to take place in a training environment where the agenda is an open one. Thus, a well-trained sales force has a better spirit of comradeship and from that stems lower rates of sales force turnover.

Training programmes thus create interest and is specifically helpful to new sales personnel.

2 *Supervision of sales personnel*

This is closely related to training. There are times when only a personal exchange of views can unearth underlying doubts in the mind of an individual.

Supervision is not overseeing or criticism. Critique should be presented in a positive vein. An ability to counsel is thus of great importance as is the ability to observe deviations from accepted codes of conduct and practice. These should be corrected in a way which is instructive and positive without destroying morale.

3 *Motivation of sales personnel*

In practical terms there are two forms of reward that influence a sales person's motivation:

(*i*) *Internal rewards.* These are purely psychological and are centred on feelings of self-esteem and accomplishment. When a long-held goal is attained or a belief vindicated, that brings reward in its own right. Others, however, may be unaware of these goals. It is thus possible that a manager cannot influence the setting of such goals other than to suggest to the sales person that it might be a good idea to have them.

(*ii*) *External rewards.* These are much more likely to be tangible (e.g. sales or profit related income, prizes or perks). These are rewards for attainment of goals set by the organisation which may be totally different to the goals set by the individual.

There is a positive link between job satisfaction and motivation. Conflicting demands of superiors make goals unclear and motivation will suffer. If goals are unclear or unspecified the individual relies upon his or her own internal goals. Even attainment of these internal goals is unlikely to lead to job satisfaction. Self-esteem is not the same as the esteem (and reward) expressed by others.

4 *Recommendations for AV sales personnel*

Observations

1 Clearly, there are conflicts between what individuals see as their goals and what is necessary from the company's point of view. The lack of direction shown has led to five out of six representatives setting their own goals and specializing in their own product presentations. As long as they attain overall targets, nobody seems to have troubled them.

2 The net result has been a disregard for market potential. Profit opportunities might well have been missed because nobody kept account of where the company was proceeding in the marketplace, so much so that other smaller companies are gaining a competitive advantage. The company has perhaps understood the marketplace, but it has not used this understanding to best effect.
3 Individuals have developed their own skills in specific areas.

Recommendations

1 As Extrudaline is being sold most successfully in those areas that do not necessarily offer most potential, its specific promotion should be contemplated in potentially better areas.
2 An investigation should be undertaken to ascertain whether or not the sales force is under strength. Clearly, many more opportunities exist as sales are supervised in a haphazard way. Vickers should ask Horne to use his marketing research expertise to resolve this problem.
Since individuals have developed their own skills in specific areas this should be used to advantage and a series of sales seminars should be set up to promote an exchange of views where salespeople can learn from each other.
4 In order to assess basic training needs more fully, Vickers must spend more time in the field and then report his recommendations back to Horne.
5 Targets should be set with regard to market potential and not past performance. Effective measures to assess market share must be implemented. Targets should, in the short term, encourage a balance across the product spectrum of the company.
6 It might be necessary to increase the size of the sales force in time. However, the short-term need is for consolidation in each territory. Functional or market specialization will then follow.

Conclusion

Again, you will see that the suggested solutions are more than you could have written in one and a half hours, but you should have incorporated some of the ideas and structures into your own solutions. You will also note that there is no specific report style and we have adopted different styles in answering these questions. The best advice we can give here is to find a style that suits you and keep to this as long as that style is clear and breaks the problem down into a number of discrete component parts. The style should be readable and set out in such a way as to make your answer easy for the examiner to mark. Thus, one point should logically follow the other within a main heading and when there is a new theme, this should call for another main heading.

This concludes that part of the book where full suggested solutions are provided. The next chapter allows you to practise mini-case answering technique without full guidance.

8

MINI CASES WITH GUIDANCE ON ANSWER STRUCTURES

The purpose of this final chapter is to give you practice in solving mini-case problems. We have provided guidance on how to answer examination questions so that you can check your answers against our suggested approach. More to the point, it will give you the opportunity to apply what you have learned from this text.

All the mini cases in this chapter have been taken from the Chartered Institute of Marketing's December sittings and fully worked suggested solutions produced by examiners are not available.

Budget your time carefully to 90 minutes per mini case including reading time. You start with two certificate mini cases covering the practice of sales management and the practice of marketing December 1988 examinations.

As has been pointed out throughout the text, many students fail through misinterpretation of the questions set, so hopefully the guidance that comes after each of the cases will help you to avoid such misinterpretations in the actual examination.

PRACTICE OF SALES MANAGEMENT

December 1988

Part A: Read the following case and then answer *both* questions.

Industrial Aggregates Limited

Frank Fielding, the Regional Sales Manager for Yorkshire and Humberside has been experiencing problems of ensuring the company actually had stocks to fulfill the orders that his sales force had obtained. There seemed no way of knowing which kinds of stock were available, and which were not.

There was then the problem of servicing key accounts when overall stocks might be at a low level as some customers were more important than others. For the purpose of retaining those key customers it was vital that they were given priority. (See bar chart.) Some of his sales force did not seem to appreciate how or why the firm was low on stocks of particular types at certain times of the year. They did not seem to understand that they could not sell what they wanted to sell, but had to ration their output.

Being a major supplier to the construction industry meant that they had to stock comparatively few lines of materials, but each in rather large quantities, for example:

- Crushed sandstone, for use as hardcore in building foundations, and laying pathways and roads.
- Crushed limestone, sometimes used as hardcore, but also sold to the steel making and chemicals industries.
- River sand, and pebbles, for concrete making.
- Building sand, for cementing.

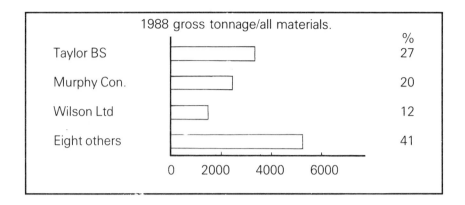

Building materials are, by their very nature, heavy and bulky. That makes them expensive to transport. For that reason, national building concerns do not buy centrally, but as close to their particular sites as is practically possible.

Much of Industrial Aggregates custom, therefore, comes from the national building concerns. That includes those who are more closely associated with civil engineering contracts than with housebuilding. Civil engineers, however, tend to do most of their work in concrete, whereas the housebuilding sector uses small amounts of concrete for foundations. They also use larger amounts of crushed sandstone for drives and the roads they lay on new estates. Housebuilders also use large amounts of building sand for cement making.

Industrial Aggregates Ltd sales force

The Yorkshire and Humberside region has four salesmen, each with a separate territory. They are all paid a low basic salary with a company car and mileage allowance, but each depends on commission earnings, which is currently 1.5 per cent of order value.

Each is able to offer discounts of up to 5 per cent on any deal without losing commission. Most of the sales force offer discounts on all large orders and, in order to attract as much business as possible, tend to offer discounts on virtually all orders.

Supply of materials

The company is supplied mainly by rail from a small number of quarries and excavation sites. Demand is seasonal, with building and construction work coming to a virtual standstill during winter. Supply is also affected by the climate. There is the problem of ice and snow in winter, but severe downpours can flood quarries and make them inaccessible when demand is often at its peak.

This can lead to important orders being delivered late, and the possibility of penalty clauses has been raised by some of the larger contractors, thus making logistics a real cause for concern.

Questions

Part A: Answer both of the following questions. Each question carries *equal* marks.

Time allowed: 90 minutes

1 What, if anything, is wrong with the existing commission structure, and why do you think it has an effect on the ability of Fielding to service key accounts properly?
   How would you change it? (*20 marks*)
2 Fielding is thinking of sending each of his sales force on a business appreciation course in order to gain a fuller insight to the company's requirements. What do you think such a course should emphasize, bearing in mind the details of the situation? (*20 marks*)

Answers to questions – *Industrial Aggregates Limited*

1 What, if anything, is wrong with the existing commission structure, and why do you think it has an effect on the ability of Fielding to service key accounts properly?
   How would you change it?
2 Fielding is thinking of sending each of his sales force on a business appreciation course in order to gain a fuller insight to the company's requirements. What do you think such a course should emphasize, bearing in mind the details of the situation?

Question 1 gives you the opportunity to say that nothing is wrong (insertion of 'if anything' into the question). This would be a route to failure! A lot is wrong, and this is what must be pointed out in an answer. In fact, the latter part of this question – why do you think it has an effect on the ability of Fielding to service key accounts – confirms that the examiner thinks that there is something wrong.

The second part of Question 1 asks for your prescription – how would you change the commission structure? Although no division of marks is given within this first question it would be fair to assume that it would be half for the first part and half for the second part.

Question 2 is more straightforward and simply asks for your opinion as to what should be included in a business appreciation training course. It does end, however, by stating 'bearing in mind the details of the situation' – so ensure that what you recommend is situation specific to the actual case and not just a general listing that could apply to any situation. Remember that a common criticism of examiners is that many students tackle mini cases and produce answers that could relate to any situation. In other words, they answer it without any regard (or application) to the case situation.

In your answer you should address the following:

1 'If anything' (is wrong). There is plenty wrong, so commence with a positive statement to this effect. Then go on to list what is wrong with the commission structure (all of which is very obvious).
2 Why do you think it has an effect (i.e., a negative effect) on the ability of Fielding to service key accounts? This is really a matter of taking the points you have picked out already and providing some justification for them. You can do this separately or, better perhaps, justify each one as the list of points are made. This will also allow you to write it up in more of a report style structure – which is what is preferred in mini-case answers.
3 'How would you change it?' This asks you to prescribe a possible solution – having identified the problems in the first part of the first question. There are a number of possible solutions, but the point that should be made is that low basic and (relatively) high commission is not a recipe for fostering customer loyalty. The fact that the 'discretionary' 5 per cent discount (i.e., without loss of commission) means that in effect all orders are discounted and this will lose the company money needs to be highlighted, and a possible solution prescribed.
4 'What do you think such a course (on business appreciation) should emphasize?' This one must be situation specific – so a mere checklist of what is in a typical business appreciation course will not do.

The sales force clearly do not understand the pricing/costing mechanisms (automatically offering 5 per cent discount) and the implications this will have on the cash flow of the company. Clearly, some kind of financial appraisal course is necessary. One could argue similarly for other aspects of the business – remembering to give justification for each element in the course.

PRACTICE OF MARKETING

December 1988   (*40 marks*)

Appleton Training Centre

Section 1

Appleton Training Centre (ATC) was established ten years ago to provide short (one- to five-day) non-qualification courses for the training and development of managers and executives.

In the ten years since it was started, ATC has been moderately successful and there has been a steady, though not spectacular, improvement in both revenue and profits. A policy of re-investing any trading surpluses has been pursued and as a consequence the centre can now boast of four purpose-built lecture rooms, eight syndicate rooms and eighty study bedrooms, each with its own en-suite bathroom. There is a small bar and a comfortable lounge area where course members can relax together at the end of the day. To support this size of operation there is a well appointed dining room and kitchen plus the usual administrative support functions. The current comprehensive range of management courses are staffed by freelance trainers who work for ATC on the basis of a fee per course.

Running such an establishment is never easy, particularly when, as is often found, the level of demand can fluctuate quite erratically. One week, because of the lack of customers, it may be operating at, or near, break-even, while the following week it is having to turn customers away because of the limitations imposed by the lecture room and bedroom facilities.

Although nationally the demand for management training and development courses is strong, competition is becoming increasingly difficult. More companies are moving into the business, often with a specific focus to their activities such as sales/marketing, accounting/finance, production and personnel/people management. Many of the newer organizations have invested heavily in their accommodation and an increasing number are now providing a range of recreational facilities such as squash courts, tennis courts, putting green, sauna, multi-gym, TV lounge, etc.

The management of ATC have recognized that, for them to be able to continue to run the centre at a consistently high level of occupancy, they must be able to match, or better, the competition in meeting the demands from industry and commerce.

Questions

Part A: Answer *both* of the following questions. Each question carries equal marks. Time allowed: 90 miutes

1 Prepare and justify an annual promotional plan for ATC.
2 What marketing information is needed by ATC's management in running the business and how should they collect this information?

Appleton Training Centre (ATC)

1 Prepare and justify (*1*) an annual promotional plan (*2*) for ATC.
2 What (*3*) marketing information is needed (*3*) by ATC's management in running the business and how should they collect this information? (*4*)

The questions appear to be separate and distinct and we can assume that one does not relate to the other, although in practice we would anticipate Question 2 preceding Question 1. It is quite appropriate to answer these questions in either order.

The ATC case study gives us virtually no clues on promotion or marketing information held but the following key points are pertinent:

(*a*) ATC have survived ten years in business.
(*b*) It is a relatively small scale operation in a buoyant market although facing the threat of progressive competition.
(*c*) Capacity utilization suffers peaks and troughs so therefore promotional activity should be designed to even out the trade cycle – possibly by appropriate targeting.
(*d*) Assumptions should be made on location of the business and for the size of the promotional spend – however modest.
(*e*) Promotion alone will not match the facilities provided by competitors so this can only be considered as a short-term tactical device to increase ATC occupancy levels.

The following points should be noted in preparing an answer structure:

1 Prepare *and* justify. Students must not only outline their suggestions in a structured promotional plan across a 12 month period but also justify the approach to be taken. This is quite demanding for the time allocated and therefore in-depth treatment will not be expected.

2 <u>Annual promotional plan</u>. The essential contents of the plan however would be:

  (*a*) Assumptions upon which to base the play,
  (*b*) Objectives to be achieved within 12 months,
  (*c*) Target groups for the promotion,
  (*d*) Media selection and justification,
  (*e*) Below-the-line activity and justification,
  (*f*) Publicity and justification,
  (*g*) Contingency action in the event of non-fulfilment,
  (*h*) Methods to review the plan,
  (*i*) Suggested budget level and breakdown,

3 <u>What is needed</u>. This requires a simple marketing information specification. But what is needed will have to be based upon the nature of marketing decisions to be taken – assumptions will be needed for these.

4 <u>How should they collect this information?</u> Well, simply the means of data collection related to the information specification is all that is required.

For Question 2, owing to time constraints, we would suggest three columns:

1	*2*	*3*
Assumptions on marketing decisions to be made.	Information needed to process decisions.	Sources of information and means of collection.

There now follow six cases from the Chartered Institute of Marketing's Diploma examinations. These concentrate more upon strategic issues and require a more structured type of answer than those of the certificate examinations. All of these mini cases are from November/December sittings and, again, specimen answers do not exist. We have, however, suggested answer structures which can be consulted at the end of each mini case.

Again, limit yourself to 90 minutes per mini case, including reading time.

MARKETING MANAGEMENT – PLANNING AND CONTROL
Time: 1½ hours　　　　　　　　　　　　　　　November 1987

AAA Adagency

AAA Adagency are an advertising agency originating in a large London suburb. Formed in 1964 by George Adkin and Brian Atkinson, AAA grew to become the largest agency in the area and one of the largest independent agencies outside the city boundary. Both George Adkin and Brian Atkinson had previously worked in small agencies: George as an account executive (sales) and Brian as copywriter having successfully completed a course in journalism following his graduation at the local polytechnic with a degree in business studies.

Many of George's previous agency clients switched to AAA when formed, owing to close personal relationships and George's creative flair. More and more clients were gained mainly from the textile industry with a particular emphasis upon mens' clothes and soft furnishings manufacturers and mail order companies. Obviously more staff had to be employed as the agency grew and eventually departments were formed including sales (account directors and executives), production, creative artists, copywriters, media analysts and administration (finance, secretaries, reception, etc.).

In 1974 George agreed to buy Brian out to enable him to move into publishing, and AAA moved offices nearer to the heart of the city to a new multi-storey building with fine views over the river and historic buildings.

Since 1974 AAA gradually became more research-orientated and in 1984 employed a full-time market researcher to help in developing campaigns for both existing and prospective new clients.

It is claimed that UK companies tend to change their advertising agencies once every five years and when changing usually brief at least three other agencies who then 'pitch' competitively for the account. The pitch (or presentation) for a prospective important new client's advertising account can cost an agency several thousand pounds, since it includes the cost of research into the client's market, the production of colour visuals to illustrate the creative ideas generated, mock-ups of POS display material, leaflet scamps and of course the time of senior directors. Bearing in mind an average of a one-in-four chance of gaining an account, the necessary business of continually making pitches becomes quite expensive and time consuming.

AAA currently enjoy the patronage of about thirty accounts, five of which are small companies, five large and twenty medium-sized. The total amount of billings (turnover) for the year ended April 1987 was about £25 million. One account executive services the five small accounts, nine account executives look after the twenty medium-sized accounts and five account directors individually service the five largest accounts with at least a monthly visit to discuss the advertising aspects of their client's marketing efforts and to present new creative ideas for consideration. About one third of the total staff of 120 people work on administration.

AAA like many other agencies do not plan long-term. Owing to the turning over of accounts and the constantly changing advertising expenditure of individual clients, forecasting is extremely difficult. Because of these factors AAA express their objectives in terms of a minimum profit target rather than a given turnover. Apart from commission from the media for space booked on behalf of their clients, AAA make profit on a cost-plus basis from the design and provision of various forms of promotional literature and POS display material. AAA also offer exhibition/fashion show design services but do not engage in such below-the-line services as the design of incentive schemes or PR campaigns. AAA do not offer marketing research facilities to their clients, their market researcher being used for internal purposes only.

AAA are not therefore a full-service agency at this stage in their development and prefer to recommend outside specialists rather than sub-contract requests for services outside their normal portfolio.

Questions

1 How would the process of frequently having to pitch for new accounts affect marketing planning and control procedures within the agency?
2 In 1986 AAA lost its largest account but gained an even larger account in 1987 – that of a significant retail showroom chain specializing in consumer durables. Outline the adjustments in internal resourcing and agency planning and control procedures considered necessary in endeavouring to accommodate these changes.

Both questions carry equal marks.

AAA Adagency

1 How would the process *(1)* of frequently having to pitch for new accounts affect marketing planning and control procedures *(2)* within the agency?

There are two points of emphasis in this question:

1 Process.
2 Procedure.

It is important to recognize that marketing planning is a management function involving organization, coordination, evaluation, control and decision making.

The organization culture within the AAA Adagency is one of management by crisis. The process of frequent pitching is indeed disruptive, which means that time for future planning is rarely sacrosanct.

The emphasis on process must focus upon the business as a human resource activity centre operating under conditions of tension with competing demands upon management time.

Procedures for marketing planning and control suggest the need for systematic regular periods for planning ahead and reviewing performance. It would be appropriate to state the typical procedures involved and then stated how difficult it would be to achieve these in the dynamic environment of an overloaded advertising agency operating under considerable pressure.

2 In 1986 AAA lost *(1)* its largest account but gained *(1)* an even larger account in 1987 – that of a significant retail showroom chain specializing in consumer durables *(2)*. Outline *(3)* the adjustments *(4)* in internal resourcing and agency planning and *(5)* control procedures considered necessary in endeavouring to accommodate these changes.

Apart from the content of the question, there are five points to pick up in order to structure a sound answer:

1 Gains and losses. Again, this supports the theme of a volatile internal environment featured in Question (1), an environment typical of the industry. A good answer would require a close identification with the prevailing business operations within AAA to demonstrate an understanding of the atmosphere of day-to-day working and the anxiety for management control.
2 The significance of this business must be identified in relation to the profile of accounts the agency holds. Comments on how this will now be handled would be wise.
3 'Outline' means just that – not an extended treatise!

4 'Adjustments' – the key word, i.e., what changes are needed to accommodate the new business? Changes to (*1*) planning and control procedures (if any) and (*2*) internal resourcing. The implications for 'no adjustments' could also be outlined.

5 'And'. The point that most students miss! The examiner will search for planning *AND* control procedures so do not overlook these.

MARKETING MANAGEMENT – PLANNING AND CONTROL
Time: 1½ hours   December 1988

Section 1: *Compulsory (carrying 50% of the marks)*

Crafted Foundry Products (CFP) Ltd

CFP, an old-established foundry in the heart of the industrial Midlands, got into difficulties in late 1985 when its major customer went into liquidation, owing considerable debts. CFP were obliged to drastically reduce their work-force and rapidly went into a loss-making situation, finding they were unable to cover fixed costs with the small amount of business coming in from remaining customers.

Early in 1986 CFP accepted a management buy-out offer by two of its most able managers: John Irons (Production Manager) and Jim Steel (Customer Relations).

Owing to over-dependence on one major customer CFP had never felt the need for a sales force or a formal Sales/Marketing Manager. However, it had two major strengths, one of which was the extremely high quality of its castings which owed much to the efforts of John Irons. The other major strength had been built up by Jim Steel in the form of a design and estimating service. This enabled potential customers to get their own rough sketches or ideas turned into design drawings by CFP for estimating purposes; CFP adding their suggestions for improvements against design/cost/installation criteria. By this means CFP had consistently been able to please customers by turning out castings of considerably higher quality/utility than customers had originally envisaged.

At the time of the buy-out offer Jim Steel was negotiating the supply of street furniture to their local city authority as part of a campaign to improve the image of the city as a tourist attraction. The street furniture designs being discussed covered litter bins incorporating the city coat of arms, 'olde-worlde' street signs, street posts and benches, finished in black and gold paint. As an additional inducement CFP were offering to finish the street furniture with a new rubber-based paint which resisted corrosion and chipping, plus a maintenance service so that the street furniture was always clean and new looking.

In 1988, CFP's position had greatly improved. Considerable orders were coming in from their local authority for street furniture, profits were being made and the work force had expanded. However, CFP still had spare production capacity at their own foundry and could, of course, subcontract casting to a number of other foundries capable of high quality work.

After attending an IM Branch Meeting where you met Jim Steel, you have accepted a part-time marketing consultancy contract for the next twelve months for CFP. After completing Situational/SWOT analyses, CFP have decided upon a corporate objective of steady profitable growth using the company's product and service strengths to build up a stronger customer base, i.e., a combined strategy of product and market development.

Questions

1 Draw up an outline *tactical* plan to fulfil these strategies.
2 What controls would you incorporate in your tactical plan?

Both questions carry equal marks.

Crafted Foundry Products Ltd

(1) Draw up a <u>tactical plan (*1*)</u> to <u>achieve these strategies (*2*)</u>.

Two points emerge from Question 1:

1 A <u>tactical plan.</u> Be sure that a tactical plan is produced and not a strategic plan. This means that it is necessary to get down to operational level. Decide the tasks needed to achieve specified objectives. Work out the precise timing of these tasks and schedule these within a one-year framework. Determine how the tasks are to be actioned, by whom and where and set up a system for review.
2 <u>To achieve these strategies.</u> What strategies? Return to the case to make sure you are clear on what strategies have been determined, i.e., a combined strategy of product and market development. Now ensure that the tactical plan is tailor made to achieve the stated strategies. Therefore it is essential to use the product base and market bases stated in the case.

The answer should refer closely to the scenario presented in the case study.

(2) <u>What controls (*1*)</u> would you (*2*) <u>incorporate (*1*)</u> in your tactical plan?

Clearly there is now a close relationship between Questions (1) and (2). The more adventurous student would treat the answer using a broadsheet.

In such a way Questions 1 and 2 would be presented as an integrated whole. However, for the more conventional there are two parts to acknowledge and respond to:

1 <u>What controls?</u> Controls can be divided into quantitative controls and qualititative controls and should be itemized for each level of your tactical plan. I would suggest the word 'incorporate' means that it is essential to tailor your controls to the tasks you have specified in Question 1.
2 <u>Would you.</u> 'Would you' can be disregarded as a simple question, but oh no, do not fall into this trap. 'Would you' raises the covert question – why? This must not be left unanswered. What is therefore required is a justification for your proposed controls.

   Therefore what is required is a set of qualitative and quantitative controls linked to each part of your tactical plan – and a justification for them.

Do not think that these are simple direct questions requiring simplistic answers – far from it.

MARKETING COMMUNICATIONS

Time: 1½ hours   November 1987

Section 1

Laser Cards

Credit cards in 1987 are in acknowledged worldwide use as the convenient alternative to money for a variety of financial transactions. In very recent times this type of plastic card has been developed to store information – just like a microcomputer.

Today COMTEC, one of Britain's major communications companies, revealed plans to introduce a new card, the Callup Card, which will be ready for market launch by their national sales force in 1989.

The Callup Card has been developed on a new plastic material onto which information can be transferred by a special heat sensitive photographic process. The card, just six centimetres by four centimetres, can store up to 1000 pages of typed information.

COMTEC have also, in prototype form, a special machine to enable users of the card to read information as well as to write more data on to it, by using a low powered laser – hence the in-house code name, 'Laser Card'.

COMTEC anticipate a wide variety of end-use applications for the Callup Card because it is up to fifteen times cheaper than similar cards now on the market which have a microchip built into them. The laser technology supersedes the microchip cards which competitors currently market.

Following product trials in the United States and Japan, COMTEC are starting trials in January 1988 to discover the best way to develop and exploit the UK market.

Market research conducted in the UK has identified several key areas.

In the medical field, patient records have been suggested; in the banking area, banks' and building societies' records of deposits and withdrawals; for the restricted personnel zones, the card would be used as an electronic key and then form part of a complex identification system; for publishers, detailed records, books, technical manuals, etc. can be stored; in the field of industrial manufacturing, complex processes could be recorded; in the aircraft industry detailed up-to-date information on servicing and maintenance is vital to the safe performance of all aircraft.

By 1989 the cost of each card will be £5 and the laser machine which reads and writes the cards will be just less than £1,000.

What now remains to be seen is whether, following market research and field trials, these industry segments will choose the Callup Card. As yet no limit has been set for the promotional budget.

Questions

1 Outline essential marketing communications tasks facing COMTEC for the 1989 Callup Card launch. (*25%*)
2 Recommend a suitable marketing communications strategy to achieve these tasks. (*75%*)

Laser Cards

1 Outline (*1*) essential (*2*) marketing communications tasks (*3*) facing COMTEC for the 1989 Callup card launch (*4*).

More to this question than meets the eye! Four dimensions are clear:

1 'Outline'. This means precisely what it says – not a treatise, not a situational analysis, but a simple statement of 'what' needs to be done.
2 'Essential'. This word has been chosen deliberately. The covert, and hence subjective, question implicit here is: 'Why are these tasks essential?' There can be no debate verbally so therefore it must occur on the answer book, i.e., a simple justification as to why these tasks specified are essential in your view.
3 'Tasks', i.e., *what* has to be done. This may be another way of the examiner asking you for objectives, but a task is something more immediate in nature and suggests a more tactical approach to the launch of the callup card.
4 The 1989 Callup card launch. The brief now is quite clear. The boundaries for the exercise are just the launch. However, 1989 suggests a time scale, so now the tasks become time dependent, i.e, maybe before, during and even after the Callup card launch.

Note: Only 25 per cent of your effort to Question 1.

2 Recommend (*1*) a suitable marketing communications strategy to achieve these tasks (*2*).

A more general question. The answer will however depend upon how well the tasks have been outlined in Question 1. Note the need for integration between Questions 2 and 1.

There are two angles to be covered:

1 Recommend – and by implication, justify. This means suggesting clear courses of action and defending them.
2 Strategy to achieve these tasks. An assumption here may be helpful that you assume strategy to be the means by which the tasks are to be achieved. If tasks are the 'what' then strategy is the how and when and where within identified constraints, particularly budgetary. The boundaries to the term marketing communications strategy need to be defined. Therefore, again assumptions are recommended to support the approach you will propose.

Under Question 1 target audiences should have been selected and given priority. The communications strategy therefore is the means by which these groups will be reached through using the elements of the promotional mix. A strategy subsumes review, so means for control, review and effectiveness evaluation should be included in the answer.

Time: 1½ hours   December 1988

Gordon's of Stirling

The United Kingdom confectionery market is estimated to be worth £3 billion in 1988, exactly 10 per cent of that total being sold in Scotland.

Chocolate products are bought, in general, either for self-indulgence (Kit Kat, Mars Bars) or as a gift (Black Magic, All Gold). Price seems to play an important part in brand choice, people being much more cost-conscious when buying for themselves.

Against this background, Gordon's of Stirling are in the process of re-launching themselves and their single main product. Founded in Dundee in 1850 by William and Mary Gordon, the company moved to Stirling at the turn of the century and was acquired by one of Britain's 'big four' chocolate firms in 1927.

The new owner used the Stirling factory to expand its presence in an increasingly lucrative and competitive confectionery market. The Gordon's product line continued until 1966, when the family firm was absorbed entirely into its parent company. In 1986, the parent withdrew from Scotland altogether.

A team of former employees has decided to re-enter the market with Gordon's original prime product, Continental Creams, made at the same factory in Stirling, now leased to them by their former employer. They believe they can earn a good return on their investment if they capture only between one and ten per cent of the Scottish market. Three new lines are planned for 1989: apricot brandy truffles, chocolate ginger pralines and orange curaçao bonbons.

Managing Director Don Dalziel is well aware that he cannot compete on equal terms with the giants of the chocolate business. He has set the maximum feasible promotional budget at £10,000 for year one, for instance. So he has decided to aim for a market segment demanding a quality product of clearly Scottish origin. Market research findings suggest that there is a gap in the Scottish market for such a brand and that none at present available is perceived to be distinctly Scottish.

Kenneth Colquhoun, Sales and Marketing Director, a major-accounts sales manager with Gordon's for fifteen years, believes people are today ready to pay a premium price for something genuinely different. He proposes to major on the gift appeal of the re-launched product. Black Magic, for instance, costs about £1.78 for a 227-gram box.

Recognizing that packaging matters as much as the product itself in such a market, he has commissioned a totally new pack from Scotland's leading design house. Avoiding the tartan-and-heather theme of many Scottish goods, it is a clean and simple design in dark red, cream and dark blue. The assortment of six dark-chocolate cream centres (orange, gooseberry, raspberry, apricot, lime, blackcurrant) seems to show through a window while a band around the middle carries the new logo and the product name.

The retail price of the 62-gram assortment will be 49 pence.

Kenneth Colquhoun feels the time is right for re-launched Continental Creams for two reasons in addition to the general success of up-market brands in modern Britain. First, though most confectionery brands are bought by the 18–35 age group, a significant number of people in Scotland remember that Gordon's was 'the Scots word for chocolate'. Second, Edinburgh attracts 2.5 million tourist visitors per year.

Question

Kenneth Colquhoun now has to produce an outline marketing communications plan for the launch of Continental Creams for submission to an agency that provides assistance with marketing start-up costs, and has asked you to advise him on content and presentation.

It is essential that you attach priorities to each element of the proposed plan, allocate the promotional budget of £10,000 accordingly, and provide clear reasoning to support your recommendations.

Gordon's of Stirling

Kenneth Colquhoun (*1*) now has to produce an outline marketing communications plan (*2*) for the launch of (*3*) Continental Creams for submission to an agency that provides assistance with marketing start-up costs and has asked you (*1*) to advise him on content and presentation (*2*). It is essential that you attach priorities (*4*) to each element of the proposed plan, allocate the promotional budget of £10,000 (*5*) accordingly and provide clear reasoning (*6*) to support your recommendations.

Phew! A lot of words, and some smoke screening here, so it is essential that the question is read slowly several times to pick out the main structural elements.

To proceed, the following dimensions need to be considered:

1 Kenneth Colquhoun. Who *is* he? Who are you? Decide your role and assume the mini-case study questions 'in role'. Therefore state your assumptions: 'In my capacity as . . . .' and therefore address your plan to the designated party.

2 Outline marketing communications plan. Know this structure well before attempting an answer. Consult the Wings case study on page 63 for evidence of an acceptable format.

3 Launch. Remember the timing and marketing communications activity implications to build up and sell into the trade before selling out to the consumer.

4 Attach priorities. Do not overlook this part of the question. Priority can be time or task dependent or both; a suitable means of notation is therefore required. It would appear that weighting could be an appropriate means also of designating priority to elements of the plan. A simple allocation by percentage of the budget would again suffice to denote priority attachment.

5 A promotional budget of £10,000. Oh dear, the immediate reaction would be: 'Is this some kind of a joke?' How can the launch of a new confectionery item be achieved on such a modest sum, even within the regional environs of Scotland? You have little choice – either to challenge the question as a typographical error, and that is a dangerous strategy, or recognize that the launch has to be achieved on an extremely low budget. Then treat this as a challenge; it means little or no media spend! and lots of non-costed promotion and publicity. Perhaps there is an angle here: 'Gordon's of Stirling relaunch Continental Creams on an unsweetened budget!' Clearly the examiner will award credit for any creative stance made and penalize heavily anyone who does not recognize the reality of these budgetary constraints.

6 Provide clear reasoning. Again, justification is required for your proposed approach to the problem in hand.

INTERNATIONAL ASPECTS

Approximate time: 1½ hrs   November 1987

Section 1

Tubelites plc

Tubelites plc are electric lighting specialist manufacturers in the south of the UK. An old-established firm, they have been concerned with the development and applications of designs of fluorescent tube lights for both domestic and industrial use; and more recently, in the design and manufacture of specialist lighting effects for outdoor display purposes. Their basic product consists of a glass tube, virtually of any length between one to 6 feet, and of diameters between about ¾–2 inches. This tube is coated internally with various chemicals before being filled with one of a number of gases: neon, sodium, krypton and argon being the types most commonly used. When an electric current is passed through the tube, it causes the gas to fluoresce and produce a bright light. Depending on the particular combination of chemical coating and the gas used, this light can be in reds, oranges, yellows, greens and blues, as well as various shades of white according to design requirements.

While the basic lighting tube is straight, the glass can be formed in different shapes when molten, allowing a design to be developed. With different shapes and colours, together with suitable switches and circuits to switch parts on and off as required, a display can be produced for use at night, which can be very striking, and give the impression of action and movement. Such displays are widely used outside shops and in public places as a form of outdoor advertising, and the basic technology to do so is widely known round the world. Tubelite's strength lay in its advanced technical expertise, firstly on its ability to combine particular coatings and gases to give particularly subtle colours and then in its sophisticated electrical circuitry to give the desired effects.

Arising from this research strength, Tubelite had become one of the leading specialists in this area in the UK, and had recently perfected systems of miniaturization of all components, so that the displays could now be used either indoors or outdoors, and measure only inches instead of feet in size of tubes. This research had been expensive, but Tubelite expected to be able to use its leading position to obtain a good price for its miniature designs.

Some 10 per cent of their normal sized production items were bought by European customers who required particular colour subtleties and effects, but the strength of other manufacturers there precluded any effective operation. With the miniature displays, however, Tubelite felt that it had about a year's lead before any similar products could be produced, and was anxious to derive as much advantage as it could in the meanwhile to establish itself for the first time with a reasonable share of the European market.

The overseas sales to date, as indeed much of the UK business, had been obtained from direct enquiries from firms or organizations requiring such displays. Tubelite felt that there was no particular reason to alter the pattern of its UK activities, but, with the miniature range, it felt that a more positive approach would be essential to obtain the objectives of entry and market share. Tubelite now required advice.

Questions

To achieve European market penetration using a rolling market entry plan:

1 What research would need to be undertaken in respect of the initial country selected?
2 What methods would you advise Tubelite to adopt to enter these countries?
3 How would you advertise and promote the miniature range?

All questions carry equal marks.

Tubelites plc

To achieve market penetration using a rolling market entry plan (*1*):

1 What research (*3*) would need to be undertaken in respect of the initial country selected (*2*)?
2 What methods (*4*) would you advise (*5*) Tubelite to adopt to enter these countries?
3 How (*6*) would you advertise and promote the (*6*) the miniature range?

The question is structured into three parts so it is necessary to budget your time to avoid producing a weak attempt to question 3 owing to time constraints.

Points to watch out for in preparing your answer:

1 <u>Rolling market entry plan</u>. This means that incremental geographic market penetration will be achieved over a specified time scale for the European market. One country at a time may be the most appropriate means to achieve the goal of European market penetration.

2 The initial country selected. The case specifies the 'European market' and we are given few clues as to countries targeted. In the absence of further information it is essential to make an assumption (e.g., weaker countries of the European Community) and then to select and justify one country, e.g. France, on the grounds of logistic convenience.

3 <u>What research?</u> Again this is very global so it is again time to superimpose a meaningful structure.

I would favour a specification of the information needs to assist particular marketing decisions which will need to be taken and the means by which the information will be obtained.

In simple terms, ask yourself:

1 What marketing decisions have to be taken to enter, say, the French market for lighting supplies?

2 What extra information do I need to take these marketing decisions?

3 From where will I obtain it, both at home within the UK and in the specified foreign country?

Note: There is an implicit justification because the research is tailored to marketing decisions.

4 <u>What methods</u>. Simply identify the means of market entry.

5 <u>Would you advise?</u> Select and justify the means you consider most appropriate to reach, penetrate and sustain a market position within the initial country(ies) selected.

6 *How* to advertise and promote. This is clear: the emphasis is upon 'how' and not 'what'. Implicit is the need to examine restrictions and to take on board the cultural dimensions if applicable. A straightforward question, covering above- and below-the-line activity and the means to achieve it.

INTERNATIONAL ASPECTS

Time: 1½ hours   December 1988

Part 1

McDonald's Fast Food Operations

The following article appeared in a UK newspaper in January 1988:

> The McDonald's fast food chain is taking a bite at the kebab-loving Balkans.
> McDonald's foray into communist Yugoslavia is a landmark joint venture
> reminiscent of when Coke and Pepsi first quenched the thirsts of people behind
> the Iron Curtain.
>
> But unlike the franchise deals and secret recipes for Cola, McDonald's has
> handed its secrets to the Yugoslavs in the shape of a new partnership firm that
> will run the restaurants.
>
> The venture, the first of its kind in Yugoslavia, will open a McDonald's
> restaurant by February. Mr Predrag Dostanic, Managing Director of the joint
> venture firm McDonald's-Genex said, 'We think McDonald's can be a big hit in
> Yugoslavia. It's a really exciting scheme.'
>
> Genex, or General Export, is Yugoslavia's biggest trading firm and widely
> regarded as its most successful, and is now diversifying into tourism, airline
> business, hotels and food.

Mcdonald's fast food chain originated in America to cater for people in a
hurry, wanting a quick snack or meal from a limited standardized list of
hamburgers of various types, fried fish, chips and hot or cold non-alcoholic
drinks. They do not serve kebabs at all. These are a savoury meal
consisting of pieces of various meats, alternating with vegetables on a
skewer, and usually grilled over a charcoal fire. MacDonald's tightly-
controlled system provided a very fast service of freshly cooked foods, and
served in brightly-lit surroundings, and with seats and tables usually fixed
to the floor and designed for speedy clearing and cleaning. The emphasis
throughout being on speed of operation and rapid turnover of customers.

While their establishments have spread to most Western European
countries, this is the first time one has been planned to operate in

an Eastern bloc country. Elmer Eggenberger, McDonald's European executive in charge of this development, is seeking widespread advice to ensure that he is covering all the main requirements for this particular development, which he naturally hopes will spread further in the Comecon countries.

Question

Advise Elmer Eggenberger by providing him with an outline tactical marketing plan which could have been used to introduce and operate this new activity in Yugoslavia.

Your plan should include reference to:

- The basis for selecting suitable towns and sites within a town for a McDonald's branch,
- The supply arrangements for equipment and raw materials,
- The introduction and subsequent promotion of the operation,
- Any other significant areas that you consider to be relevant.

McDonald's Fast Food Operations

Advise Elmer Eggenberger (*1*) by providing him with an outline tactical marketing plan (*2*) which could have been used to introduce and operate this new activity in Yugoslavia (*3*).

Your plan should include reference to:

- The basis for selecting suitable towns (*4*) and sites within a town (*5*) for a McDonald's branch.
- The supply arrangements (*6*) for equipment and raw materials.
- The introduction and subsequent (*7*) promotion of the operation.
- Any other (*8*) significant areas you consider to be relevant.

Points to note here are:

1 Elmer Eggenberger. Who is he? A fairy tale name suggests a fairy tale reply to the case – but such humour would rarely be appreciated. However, your plan should be directed for his attention.
2 Outline tactical marketing plan. This subject has been covered in earlier comments which also would apply to the McDonald's Fast Food case study.
3 Yugoslavia. Note the country, the trading bloc, prevailing environmental factors which influence business activity, marketing infrastructures and, by implication, the distinction with the UK.

4 The basis for selecting suitable towns. Basic market selection criteria could be applied here.
5 Sites within a town. This is more specific. Criteria for fast food retail site location are now required.
6 Supply arrangements. The debate should now be raised between local sources of supply and the need to import from other countries to (*a*) establish the site and (*b*) maintain business and the quality of the fast food items.
7 Introduction and subsequent. Here the phrasing of promotional activity is essential (*a*) to launch and (*b*) to carry through, so time dimensions are needed and an appropriate use of media and promotion. This means you should be aware of the restrictions in Yugoslavia. If you do not know these then assumptions must be made upon which your recommendations can be based.
8 Any other. Well, anything else that comes to mind – that is, if you have time. Our advice is to make time by budgeting your time and effort carefully on the other questions. Candidates may either pass or fail, or be awarded a higher grade for pertinent additional comments, so where possible include these. A few comments about logistics, standardization or cultural dynamics would score bonus points.

Conclusion

We hope that this text will have provided you with some insights into the technique of handling mini-case studies. Marks allocated to mini cases in the Chartered Institute of Marketing examinations are substantial in relation to the papers as a whole, so we hope that your investment in time spent studying this text will prove to be worthwhile.

We have deliberately not given any advice upon how to write reports until this late stage because most students have their own ideas as to what a report should look like in terms of structure and content. It has not been the intention of the book to be prescriptive and this is why Chapter 9 and not Chapter 1 covers advice upon writing reports for mini-case studies. If, therefore, you are happy with your present style of report writing and as long as it is clear and succinct, and maps the reader through with the minimum of backtracking, then this is all that is required.

The next chapter covers pointers upon how to write reports for mini-case study examinations.

9

WRITING REPORTS FOR MINI-CASE STUDIES

Throughout this book it has been stressed that your answers should be in report format. You will also note from the worked examples of mini-case answers that the precise format of a report – introductions, numbering systems, use of subheadings and so on – can vary. Reports differ in length, degree of formality and format as much as they do in content. For example, in practice some reports are very short and informal, perhaps presented as a memorandum; others (although not for the mini cases) will run into thousands of words.

However, all reports have common elements and benefit from adherence to a number of simple rules in their preparation. The most important of these elements and rules are as follows:

1 Planning the report

The planning stage starts with:

- The purpose of the report,
- What is to be included,
- How it is to be presented,
- To whom it is to be presented.

At this planning stage in the actual examination the questions should be broken down into their component parts and a structure designed to ensure that each of these parts is covered in the report and that the *examiner can see that they have been covered*. Sectionalization of the report and the use of clear headings (for each separate question) will help to achieve this, but so too will starting the report with a statement of terms of reference.

2 Terms of reference

At the start of a report it is a good idea to write out the terms of reference so that you can demonstrate that you understand precisely what you have been asked to do. Terms of reference should include the following:

2.1 Who the report is for and/or by whom it has been requested. *Example*: 'At the request of the marketing manager of Bloggs plc.'
2.2 The areas to be covered (i.e., the questions. *Example*:
   - Methods of entry into overseas markets.
   - The promotional mix.
   - Pricing strategies.
2.3 The intended outcome of the report. *Example*:
   - To establish strategies for developing export markets.
   - To make proposals for a coordinated promotional campaign.
2.4 The constraints/assumptions (if any) which affect the report. *Example*:
   - Within a proposed budget for promotion of £50,000.
   or
   - In compiling the report it has been assumed that the rate of inflation will continue to be 5 per cent per annum.

3 Proposals and recommendations

Remember reports are not extended essays but concise statements which set out our thoughts simply and clearly.

In most reports, and the mini cases are no exception, it is the proposals and recommendations which are of prime interest (although clearly these must be based on sound analysis).

All proposals and recommendations should be justified, but do not bore the reader with over-complicated or in-depth analysis. For the most part, in the mini cases, any detailed calculations and analysis, if required in the report, should form part of the appendices.

4 Structuring a report

As we have noted, the conventions for structuring a report vary considerably. Here is one example of a report structure which you could use in the examinations.

4.1 *Title page*:
Title of report, to whom addressed, the date, author's name and company.
4.2 *Terms of reference*:
Resumé of terms of reference (as above).
4.3 *Contents list*:
Report structure together with the numbering system which is used throughout the report. Major headings and sub-headings would be shown indexed by page.
4.4 *The main report*:
This should include the detailed facts and recommendations contained in the report.
4.5 *Appendices*:
So that the main flow of argument is not interrupted by a mass of detail, financial and other data can be summarized or referred to in the report but attached at the end. As an alternative you could insert a *summary* of your main findings and recommendations between the title page and terms of reference. This is quite common and useful in report writing.

Above all it is important that you structure your report to achieve the following:

● The report should, as far as is possible, be interesting. Remember, the examiner will have to read dozens of these reports.
● The report should be easy to understand.
● The report should follow a logical sequence leading the reader along a particular path.

5 Presentation

Presentation is crucial for a report to be well received. Each page must be well laid out to appeal to the reader's eye.

The use of white space, headings and subheadings, indentations and report numbering systems should be applied to create maximum impact.

You do not have much time in the mini-case examination, but in any event a report should contain short, sharp sections and paragraphs.

In short, write simply, write briefly, write positively and avoid cluttering the main body of your report with elaborate diagrams, calculations, and charts and tables.

10

MINI-CASE FAILURE – HOW TO MINIMIZE IT

Much of what is said in this final chapter is basically a reiteration of what has been said already. It must, therefore, be viewed more as a summary or reinforcement.

We provide advice upon examination tactics and timing and then go on to discuss balance, volume, structure presentation and style. Finally, we offer advice upon answering the question set, and not what you would like to answer – a common cause of failure!

Tactics

Decide *before* going into the examination room whether to attempt the mini case as Part 1 of the paper first or not.

To help you settle in the examination room and to build your confidence it may be wise to handle the mini case second and devote the first one and a half hours of the three-hour paper to answering Part 2 questions. However, it is not our aim to prescribe what you should do: adopt the method with which you feel most comfortable.

Timing

Spend *only* one and a half hours on the diploma mini cases and one hour on the certificate mini cases.

Budget your time to allow time to read, time to write and time to read over. Try to avoid the race against the clock to complete the question paper.

Where there is a differential allocation of marks allocate your time accordingly.

Time yourself carefully.

Balance

Aim to produce a balanced paper with appropriate attention given to all parts of the question paper. Balance your time and your effort to gain best results.

Volume

Aim to produce an answer script of substance. Substance scores points, but avoid the tendency to waffle.

Structure

Develop structural answers and use well-conceived headings which follow a logical sequence.

Presentation

Remember packaging sells the product!

Clear layout and good presentation will increase the appeal of your answer.

Use the page to full advantage – leave gaps, create white space, underline, box out key points – these will improve the impact of your answer. Even the most illegible handwriting can be improved using these techniques to create interest on the page.

Style

Adopt report format at all times. This leads to a succinct approach with practice and enables more ideas to be covered within the time limits of the examination.

Mini Cases in Marketing

Answer the questions set

Above all the examiner is looking for an answer to the *actual* questions that have been set.

Do not superimpose pre-planned structures unless they are appropriate to the actual questions asked. Do not use marketing plans, market entry plans, sales plans, marketing communications plans, SWOT analysis, *unless these are asked for in the question.*

Answers should be tailor-made to fit the case study scenario. They should relate to the issues raised and not be remote from the situation in hand.

Answer the mini-case questions as a practitioner, not as a student of marketing.

Do not depend upon textbook material to produce academic answers. Focus your attention upon producing real world answers to the real problems with which you are faced.

Where possible, quantify your answers to ensure that your recommendations for action are not purely based upon a qualitative assessment of the situation in hand. Remember that most marketing decisions have time and cost implications.

Often you are given a role – a marketing consultant, account executive, line marketing manager or whatever. *Use this role* to answer the questions – it will help you to produce reasoned judgements and maybe even to aspire to the difficulties of implementation.

If in a role you are required to make recommendations, remember who is to do what, where, when and how and remember the rationale for it – why.

Recommendations should be supported with appropriate justification. Never leave the question 'why?' open to the examiner.

Make sure that your recommendations are within the resource capabilities of the organization(s) concerned. This means that there is a need for a realistic assessment of the company and market constraints. This may prove difficult. Therefore it is suggested that you make relevant assumptions before producing recommendations for courses of action.

Remember that many case study scenarios and the questions asked of them involve change.

Change involves people and therefore the organizational implications of your recommendations should not be overlooked. Change also has time and cost considerations. Do not overlook these.

Do not assume that all courses of action will work to achieve the stated purpose or objectives. Propose contingency actions!

Questions at this level of the Chartered Institute of Marketing examinations are rarely simplistic. Each has a set of dimensions designed to achieve objectives. Therefore you must read, read over again, then read over slowly and carefully the *actual* questions to determine the actual requirements. Then structure your answers to meet with these requirements. It is wise therefore to make assumptions before answering the question to ensure that you are on the same wavelength as the person who will assess your script. When structuring your answers make sure that your structure covers all parts of the questions set. Do not try to skirt around the real issues of the examination questions.

Remember marks are awarded for answers, not analysis. Do not waste time on analysis at the cost of not putting enough time and effort into answering the questions set.

APPENDIX

A synopsis of past mini-case questions for the Chartered Institute of Marketing Diploma in Marketing Examinations

This appendix has been included for your information and it covers planning and control, international aspects of marketing and marketing communications (in that order). The actual mini case is not included, and the purpose of this appendix is to give you a 'feel' for the type of questions you can expect to be set.

This section has deliberately been put in as an appendix as it is merely meant to serve as an information resource; it is not meant to serve any instructional purposes.

Planning and control

Example 1

After attending a CIM branch meeting where you met Jim Steel, you have accepted a part-time marketing consultancy contract for the next twelve months. After completing situational/SWOT analyses, the company have decided upon a corporate objective of steady, profitable growth using the company's product and service strengths to build up a stronger customer base, i.e., a combined strategy of product and market development.

(*a*) Draw up an outline *tactical* plan to fulfil these strategies.
(*b*) What *controls* would you incorporate in your tactical plan?

Example 2

(*a*) Use Ansoff's matrix of strategic options as a framework for identifying and evaluating *specific* ideas for the profitable expansion of the company. (*30 marks*)
(*b*) Select *one* of the strategic options developed in (*a*) and outline marketing mix plans for its achievement. (*20 marks*)

Example 3

(*a*) Outline details of the marketing plan which the business owner will need in order to operate the new venture.
(*b*) What *control* problems would confront the company in endeavouring to expand up to fifty outlets by using this franchise method?

Example 4

(*a*) Suggest suitable corporate objectives for the proposed new business venture. (*10 marks*)
(*b*) Write a brief for a marketing research plan with the aim of identifying target markets for the venture. (*15 marks*)
(*c*) Outline a promotional plan to communicate with these target audiences with a budgeted spend of only £10,000 covering the three months pre-opening and three months post-opening period. (*25 marks*)

Example 5

(a) Suggest what types of information could realistically be obtained on a limited initial budget of £5,000 which would help in creating a viable medium-term marketing plan aimed at arresting the decline of business and indicate where this data might be obtained.
(b) Indicate some of the actions which might be considered in the shorter term with a view to increasing profit from the existing resources.

Example 6

In the role of the marketing consultant, draft an initial report which:

(a) Reviews the environmental factors which are likely to impact upon the business over the next five years. (*25 marks*)
(b) Suggests objectives in light of the above review and the current company situation, which you feel are achievable over the next five years. (*10 marks*)
(c) Indicates possible courses of action to profitably increase sales in the short term within the company's current production and financial constraints and suggests how to proceed to evaluate these opportunities. (*25 marks*)

Example 7

The managing director has recently recruited you as his marketing controller to evaluate means of maintaining sales in face of a declining total market, including the following possibilities:

(a) The setting up of a national franchise-type operation in the form of shops-within-shops. Lacelike have received a tentative approach from a large department store group in Scotland whereby Lacelike would supply garments for stock on sale or return, pay the department stores' sales staff wages and the stores a commission on sales of 25 per cent.
(b) The setting up of a national team of agents who would advertise in local newspapers, then visit prospective clients to personally introduce the range, measure up and handle orders. Lacelike already have one such agent in Birmingham who has her own wedding photography and catering business.
(c) Exporting mail-order to department stores in major cities throughout the world. Lacelike have found that their wedding dresses quite often find their way to countries such as Poland, Czechoslovakia, Ghana, Nigeria, etc. via relatives and friends in Great Britain.

1 Suggest the criteria by which you would evaluate these three basic opportunities.
2 What would be the marketing planning and control implications arising out of the adoption of each of these three propositions?

Example 8

The assistant to the marketing and sales director is ambitious to make a contribution to the company's future marketing plans and is particularly concerned at the apparent vulnerability of the company, the difficulty of forecasting future sales and the lack of control over marketing operations.

In the assistant's role submit a *report* which:

(*a*) Reviews *major* current and possible future strengths, weaknesses, opportunities and threats.
(*b*) Suggests appropriate marketing strategies for the next five years.

International aspects of marketing

Example 9

As the appointed marketing consultant, advise the company upon the following:

(*a*) The information which would be needed to determine suitable countries to be possible markets.
(*b*) The methods by which this information could be gathered.
(*c*) Potential options for the distribution and promotion in the United Kingdom as an export market.

£250,000 is available for the development of this project of overseas business development within the UK.

Example 10

To achieve European market penetration using a rolling market entry plan:

(*a*) What research would need to be undertaken in respect of the initial country selected?
(*b*) What methods would you advise the company to adopt to enter these countries?
(*c*) How would you advertise and promote the miniature range?

Example 11

(*a*) What conditions would be required in selected European countries for the company to consider these as possible markets for their products?
(*b*) What criteria would determine the selection of distribution channels in a country of your choice?
(*c*) Outline a suitable promotional strategy for the company in a country of your choice.

Example 12

Advise the company upon:

(*a*) A suitable procedure to find possible market overseas for their whisky,
(*b*) An outline plan for selecting appropriate distribution channels,
(*c*) Promotional activities.

Example 13

The questions below draw attention to some international aspects of the situation, *all* of which you are required to answer. There are other aspects relevant to the possible development of the firm's activities overseas which you may wish to consider, and credit will be given for suitable observations.
  Your recommendations should cover:

(*a*) A selection of method(s) of overseas market entry, (*30%*)
(*b*) Information required to select a particular market, (*30%*)
(*c*) Proposals for publicity and promotions within a limited budget, (*30%*)
(*d*) Additional observations, (*10%*)

Example 14

Advise the managing director on:

(*a*) A research procedure which he could carry out to determine possible overseas markets and their requirements, (*35%*)
(*b*) An outline marketing plan to develop his overseas activities, (*35%*)
(*c*) Suggestions to meet production and financial requirements, (*20%*)
(*d*) Additional observations, (*10%*)

Marketing communications

Example 15

Steven Gold has seen his sales gradually decreasing over the past few years, and the crunch has now come. His parent company require him to increase his share of the inclusive tours market by 3 per cent. He has been given a budget of £2 million over the next year to do this.

Steven has a month to prepare his communication plan for presentation to the main board.

(a) List the factors he should take into account when preparing his plan, explaining briefly why these factors are important. (*15 marks*)
(b) Prepare an outline marketing communication plan, placing special emphasis on the sales end of the business. (*35 marks*)

Example 16

(a) Outline essential marketing communications tasks facing the company for the 1989 product launch, (*25%*)
(b) Recommend a suitable marketing communications strategy to achieve these tasks, (*75%*)

Example 17

Kenneth Colquhoun now has to produce an outline marketing communications plan for the product launch for submission to an agency that provides assistance with marketing start-up costs, and has asked you to advise him on content and presentation.

It is essential that you attach priorities to each element of the proposed plan, allocate the promotional budget of £10,000 accordingly, and provide clear reasoning to support your recommendations.

Example 18

St Patrick's have now decided to test market O'Hara's in the A. C. Neilsen Southern marketing region, at £5.89 for the jug-handled 750 ml oval bottle. Consequently, the promotional appropriation for a national launch has yet to be decided.

The marketing communications consultancy at which you are a client service director has been hired by St Patrick's Beverages Ltd. Terry

Quinlan has asked you to advise him on promotional strategy for the British test market of O'Hara's Original, with particular respect to:

(*i*) Target audience segmentation,
(*ii*) Outline media strategy,
(*iii*) Sales promotion and merchandising plans,
(*iv*) Methods for the assessment of effectiveness.

Example 19

The Kit-Car Manufacturers Association is considering mounting a co-operative promotional campaign on behalf of its members, and has sought your views as an independent marketing communications consultant.

Prepare a report to be circulated to member Kit-Car manufacturers for consideration at board level covering:

(*a*) The benefits that the member firms would receive by participating in such a cooperative promotional programme,
(*b*) How the level of promotional expenditure should be decided, and the basis on which costs would be borne by individual member firms,
(*c*) An outline promotional strategy which would assist the Kit-Car Manufacturers Association in gaining for its members a greater share of the car market.

INDEX

Please note that this index has been compiled within the context of examination technique. It does not include technical aspects of marketing which arise in individual cases, as this would be inappropriate. It is expected that such technical aspects will already be known from a study of marketing through other literature or courses